D1347067

Improve Your Bridge

IMPROVE
YOUR
BRIDGE

For players at all levels

Jack Nunes

Based on the
ATV Television Series

STANLEY PAUL, LONDON

Stanley Paul & Company Limited
3 Fitzroy Square, London W1

London Melbourne Sydney Auckland
Wellington Johannesburg and agencies
throughout the world

First published 1974
Second impression July 1977
© Jack Nunes 1974

Set in Monophoto Ehrhardt by
Oliver Burridge Filmsetting Ltd, Crawley, Sussex
Printed in Great Britain by litho at The Anchor Press Ltd
and bound by Wm Brendon & Son Ltd
both of Tiptree, Essex

ISBN 0 09 119331 1

Contents

Introduction

Improve Your Bridge is intended to cover much the same ground as the popular ATV series of the same name. However, it can be used as a text-book for complete beginners as the first four chapters cover the basic principles of the game and may well serve to refresh the memories of slightly more experienced players.

It would be too much to hope that all readers will be at just that point in their bridge education where they will already be completely familiar with these first chapters and yet find the remainder entirely new. It is far more likely that they will have met some, if not all, of the ideas discussed. However, I hope that the book will go some way towards clarifying their thinking and perhaps correcting any misunderstandings.

The book does not set out to cover every aspect of the game and makes no pretence to be exhaustive on any single topic. (When you think of the millions upon millions of words that have been written about bridge, in English alone, since 1928, how could it?) Instead I have singled out a selection of those areas of the game where my experience as a bridge player and teacher has shown me there are more misconceptions and imperfectly grasped ideas than any other.

To play an acceptable game of bridge can be a lasting pleasure and the more that you know about the game, the more you enjoy it.

1.   Preliminaries

Bridge is without doubt the most popular card game ever devised. It is a game for four players, and all the equipment you need is two packs of cards of different colours, some paper and pencils for scoring, a table and four chairs – items readily available in the average household. Like all great games, bridge is easy to start to learn. And once you have started, you can go on learning for the rest of your life.

It could be said that bridge is a great-grandchild of whist, and indeed the two games have features in common, particularly in the play of the cards. If you *have* played whist before you will find your experience a help, but if you have not there is no need to despair.

Bridge is played with a pack of fifty-two cards: four suits of thirteen cards each, no jokers. The suits are clubs, diamonds, hearts and spades (later on you will find that this order of suits is significant), and in each suit the cards rank upwards from the two to the ten, Jack (or Knave), Queen, King and Ace. You will note that the Ace always counts as a high card in contrast to its value in some other card games. The top five cards of any suit – the ten to the Ace – are called the *honours*.

THE PARTNERSHIP

The game is essentially one of partnerships – the two players facing one another across the table are partners. The partnerships are usually decided by cutting the cards: all four players draw a card from the pack spread face downwards on the table, and the two players who cut the highest of the four cards partner each other – the two who cut the lowest are left to play together. You may wonder what happens if, for example, three of the players draw Aces. Well, the four suits have a ranking order with spades as the highest suit, followed by hearts, diamonds and finally by clubs.

So in this case the two highest ranking Aces would play together and the lowest Ace would partner the player who drew the other card.

There are two points to make about partnerships. One is that during the whole time you are playing with a partner you are completely together from the point of view of the score. If you do something good and earn a lot of points, your partner benefits just as much. Equally (and it can happen!), if your partner does something foolish and gives the opponents a present then you lose just as much. There is no such thing as a loss or gain for an individual. The other point is that when you read bridge articles in newspapers or books (this book for example), partnerships are almost invariably referred to as North-South and East-West as in the diagram:

Don't worry, this does not mean that you cannot play bridge without a placard hung round your neck stating which point of the compass you represent! It is purely and simply a convenient way of identifying a particular hand in a diagram - it is much easier to say 'the North hand' than talk about 'the hand at the top of the diagram'.

The draw for partners also sorts out one other detail. The player who cuts the highest card of the four is the one who chooses the seats and deals the first hand. After that the deal passes clockwise round the table, so that if South dealt the first hand, it will be West who will deal the second and so on.

THE STAGES OF PLAY

There are really four separate stages to each hand that is played. They are, in order:

 1. The deal.
 2. The bidding (or auction).
 3. The play of the cards.
 4. The scoring.

Although this is the order in which events occur at the table, it will be better to deal with them slightly out of order. Otherwise it will be difficult for a complete beginner to understand what the bidding is all about before he has grasped the essentials of the play.

The deal is simple enough. You remember that the dealer is chosen by the original cut. The player on the *left* of the dealer shuffles the pack in whichever way he finds easiest. He then passes the shuffled pack, face downwards, to the player on the *right* of the dealer who cuts the cards. Then the dealer takes the prepared pack and distributes them one at a time, clockwise, starting with the player on his left. While this is being done the dealer's partner shuffles the other pack and places it to his right in readiness for the next deal. When the deal is completed (each player should now have thirteen cards), the hands are picked up and sorted into suits for convenience. Naturally enough, all four players should hold their cards so that no one else at the table can see them.

TRICKS AND TRUMPS

There are two fundamental ideas that must be thoroughly understood before you can go on to the exciting parts of the game – the concepts of *tricks* and *trumps*. If you have already played whist or a similar card game you can skip the next few paragraphs, but if you haven't – read on!

When the play of the hand takes place one of the four players starts by detaching a card from his hand and placing it face upwards in the middle of the table. The other three players in turn (clockwise round the table) also play a card from their hands and the four cards on the table constitute a *trick*. Once the first card has been led, each of the other three players *must* play a card of the same suit if he has one. There is absolutely no exception to this – if you do not have any cards in the suit that has been led, you have to contribute a card from another suit – but if possible you must follow suit. The trick is won by the player who has played the highest card in the suit led. So if West led the 8 of spades, North played the 2 of spades, East played the 5 of spades and South (with no spades in his hand) followed with the 9 of diamonds, it would be West who had won the trick with his ♠8. It is worth reminding you again that bridge is a partnership game, so that if your partner has put a

King on a trick there would be little point in your playing the Ace – the trick already belongs to your side and it would be sensible to save your Ace in the hope of winning another trick later.

When a trick is complete, a player from the side that has won it picks up the four cards and stacks them in a neat pile, face downwards, in front of him. Whichever player of your side collects your first trick is the one who carries on collecting all the tricks subsequently won by your side, and he should add them to the earlier tricks. It will be found convenient to pile them in such a way that it is easy to see at a glance exactly how many tricks have been won. As everyone started the hand with thirteen cards, there are thirteen tricks to be fought for on every deal. Sometimes the hand can be a very one-sided affair with one partnership winning twelve or even all thirteen tricks. But more often the hand will be closely fought, one side ending ahead with seven or eight tricks to their opponents' six or five.

Although you have not yet learned which of the four players leads to the first trick, *once play has started it is always the player who has won the last trick who leads first to the next one.* To start a trick the leader has complete freedom of choice as to which of his remaining cards he plays. But, as you have already learnt, once the lead to a trick has been made the other three players must follow suit if possible.

There is also the important concept of a *trump* suit. Before play starts on every hand, in some mysterious way yet to be explained, one of the four suits is chosen as trumps. And the trumps are all-powerful – even the 2 of the trump suit will beat an Ace from any other suit. However, you only have the opportunity to win a trick in this fashion if you have no cards left in the suit that has been led. Otherwise you must simply follow suit.

Suppose that a trick goes in the following fashion. West leads ♠7 and North plays ♠A (normally enough to win the trick). Now East has no spades in his hands and diamonds are trumps. He puts on ♦5 and it looks as though he is going to win the trick. But South, like East, does not have any spades left in his hand. If he discards a club or a heart it will be East's trick, but instead he may choose to play a higher trump than East's 5. If he does so, he will win the trick for his side and is said to have 'over-trumped'.

You may occasionally hear a bridge player talk of *ruffing* instead of trumping. Do not be worried; this is not a visitor from outer space but simply another word for exactly the same thing. To let you into a secret, both 'trump' and 'ruff' are corruptions of 'triumph' from an old card game of that name.

BIDDING FOR TRUMPS

In whist the trump suit for each hand is chosen very simply. The dealer turns up his last card or another pack is cut to show a card. However, in bridge the business of choosing the trumps is very much more sophisticated. In effect the four players bid, as though in an auction, in an attempt to buy the right to name the trump suit. Unlike a real-life auction sale the players can only make bids in turn and, just like everything else in bridge, this goes clockwise round the table. Furthermore, the player who dealt the cards has to make the first bid.

Just suppose that South, the dealer, has a nice looking hand with plenty of high cards that are likely to win tricks, and more cards in spades than in any other suit. It is clearly in his interest to play the hand with spades, his long suit, as trumps. After all, the trumps are potential trick winners and the more of them that you have the better your chances. South would start things off by making a bid of 'One Spade'. That is all, just the words 'One Spade' – don't fall into bad habits and say 'I think I'll bid One Spade' or 'I shall open One Spade'. Mannerisms of this sort are irritating to the other players and should be avoided at all costs.

Now, when South bids One Spade he is not saying that he thinks he can make one trick if spades are trumps – that would be too easy! No, his opening bid of One Spade suggests that he, *with his partner's co-operation*, can make six plus *one* (seven) tricks if he is allowed to choose the trump suit. In the same way a bid of Three Diamonds would express a belief that (with partner's help) a player could make six plus *three* tricks if diamonds were trumps. Equally, a bid of Seven Clubs would suggest that the partnership hoped to take six plus *seven* (all thirteen) tricks with clubs as trumps – what is spoken of as a grand slam and clearly an ambitious call. That, of course, would be the limit – there are only thirteen tricks to play for and no one can make a bid of more than seven.

After South's supposed bid of One Spade it is West's turn to speak. It could be that he has a fair hand with a lot of Hearts. He would far prefer to play with his suit as trumps rather than with South's spades. But he is participating in an *auction* sale. If a grandfather clock was being sold and the first bid had been one of £10, you couldn't offer £5 to the auctioneer, nor make another bid of £10. You have to increase the bid or hold your peace. If West wants to bid his hearts he must say *Two* Hearts, increasing the level of the bid. Of course, if he is not hopeful of his side achieving eight tricks with hearts as trumps he does not have to join in. In that case he says 'No Bid'. ('Pass' is an acceptable alternative but 'No Bid' is more frequently used in this country.) Perhaps he does say Two Hearts; now it is North's turn to speak. He may have a long diamond suit and knowing that his partner has a hand good enough to start things off (South has made what is called an *opening bid*) he has the same sort of choice – he can bid 'Three Diamonds' or say 'No Bid'.

The auction continues round and round the table until three players in succession say No Bid.

Your first thought may be that the auction will tend to get to high levels very quickly. That is not quite true, for you remember the suits have a *ranking* order with clubs as the lowest ranking suit, diamonds next, then hearts and finally spades as the highest ranking suit. (The ranking order can easily be remembered because the initial letter of each suit is in ascending order alphabetically: **C-D-H-S**.) This means that a bid of One Diamond is a higher call than a bid of One Club. The auction could start:

South	West	North	East
1♣	1♦	1♥	1♠

each bid being higher than all the preceding ones. But if South wanted to bid his clubs again, on the second round of the auction, he would have to bid Two Clubs in order to outdo East's One Spade. You could think of all the possible bids arranged as a ladder with the lowest rung labelled One Club and running 1♣, 1♦, 1♥, 1♠, 2♣, 2♦, 2♥, 2♠, 3♣ ... up to 7♥, 7♠ – the top rung. As the auction proceeds, once a bid has been made, all subsequent bids must come from higher up the ladder.

However, there is one more possibility that has not yet been discussed. In addition to playing a hand with any one of the four suits as trumps, it can also be played in a *no-trumps* contract, shown as NT. That means just what it says – when a hand is played in no-trumps there is no trump suit; every trick is won on merit, and if you have no cards in the suit that has been led you have absolutely no choice but to make a discard from some other suit with no chance of winning the trick. As far as the bidding is concerned, no-trumps is higher ranking than all the suits. So the ladder of possible bids suggested above should really look like this: 1♣, 1♦, 1♥, 1♠, 1NT, 2♣, 2♦ . . . 7♥, 7♠, 7NT, with Seven No-trumps as the highest possible call.

Although we have not discussed the scoring so far, one point should be made quite clear. In general, you do not bid anything that you do not think your side will have a fair chance of making. If you go too high and are left to play in your contract, it will be a very expensive business if you fail by too many tricks. As you have seen, if you and your partner bid to a contract of, say, Four Hearts, you expect to be able to make ten tricks if you are allowed to play with hearts as trumps. If you succeed in making ten or more tricks you will score points for your side, but if you fall short of your target you will score nothing at all and it will be the opponents who score points. And the more tricks by which you fail, the more expensive will be the penalty incurred. Apart from hoping that the opposition get too high, the only way of scoring points for your side is to bid your way to a contract and make the appropriate number of tricks (although it never does any harm to make an extra trick or two, referred to as *overtricks*).

LEARNING BRIDGE VERNACULAR

With some idea as to how the bidding goes, it will be as well to introduce a few of the terms and new ideas involved in the play of the hand. Suppose that the bidding has gone like this:

South	West	North	East
1♠	2♦	2♥	3♦
3♠	4♦	4♠	NB
NB	NB		

It is clear that North–South have bought the contract with their bid of Four Spades. They play the hand with spades as trumps, but they have to try to make ten tricks (six plus the four that they have bid). Now both North and South have bid spades as the auction proceeded, but South was the player who *first mentioned the suit*, or introduced the idea of playing with spades as trumps. This means that South is the player who is going to do most of the work on this particular hand – he becomes the *declarer*. If North had said No Bid on the last round of the bidding, it would have been West who was declarer in a contract of Four Diamonds, for he was the East–West player to mention the diamonds first.

You will recall that earlier on the question as to which player led to the first trick was shelved. Now it can be resolved. After the bidding has finished and the declarer has been decided, it is the player on the left of the declarer who makes the opening lead, after which declarer's partner spreads his entire hand, face upwards, on the table with trumps on his right. From this point on he becomes known as the *dummy* and has no further part in the play of the hand – the declarer is in sole charge of the cards in his own hand and the cards in dummy. Dummy can light a cigarette, admire the blonde at the next table, or go and fetch the drinks according to his wont. At no time during the play of the hand should he give any hints to the declarer as to what he (the dummy) thinks is the best play. Nor should he look at his partner's hand or either of his opponent's cards. The term 'dummy' is very descriptive!

After the opening lead has been made and dummy's cards exposed, declarer leans forward and plays a card from the table. Then, after his right-hand opponent has followed, declarer plays a card from his own hand. He does twice as much work as anyone else at the table for the duration of the time he is declarer. Mind you, this does not disturb the usual rules as to which hand leads to the next trick. If it is a card from dummy that has won the previous trick, the declarer must take great care that he starts the play to the next trick by leading a card from dummy. Similarly, if he won the last trick in his own hand, the first lead to the next trick must come from hand rather than the dummy. With declarer and dummy chosen for a particular hand, the other two players are referred to as *defenders* – their aim in life will be to make enough tricks to defeat declarer's contract. They have no other chance of scoring any points on that particular deal.

In the next few chapters we will talk about just what you need to open the bidding, rather than say No Bid; we will discuss the choice of opening bid when a hand presents more than one alternative; and we will consider on what type of hand a player might want to bid no-trumps (and why!) instead of suggesting a suit. Before that is discussed, however, it will be sensible to say a little about the scoring at bridge, so that you will have some idea as to what the object of the whole exercise is. The scoring at bridge has an unfortunate reputation – it looks a great deal more complicated at first sight than it really is, and as a result has put more people off the game than any other single factor. Take heart from an old saying – that even if you do not know all the scoring details there is no need to worry, for one of the other three players is sure to know! Nevertheless, it pays to know just what it is that your side is aiming for when you bid.

2.   Scoring

When you start to play with your partner, your object is to win what is called the *rubber*. And the rubber is won by the side that first makes two *games*. It is just like a three set tennis match – you can win by two games to nil, or after reaching one all you can win the decider. To make a game you and your partner have *to bid and make a contract or contracts scoring 100 or more points*.

For a contract in spades or hearts (termed the *major suits*) you score 30 points for each trick that you make (after discounting the six that every contract starts from). So if you and your partner bid and make Three Hearts you would score 90 points (3 × 30) – referred to as a part-score, and leaving you in the position of needing only another 10 points to complete your game; if you bid and make Four Spades you would score 120 points (4 × 30) and would in fact have made a game as well.

For a contract in diamonds or clubs (the *minor suits*) you score only 20 points for each trick bid and made. So if you played in Three Diamonds and duly made the nine tricks required for your contract you would score 60 points; if you bid and made Five Clubs you would score 100 points (and a game).

Note that to score these points towards a game you must both *bid* and *make* the appropriate number of tricks. It is no good *bidding* Four Spades if you only collect nine tricks – you will have failed to make your contract and your side will have scored nothing at all. Equally, if you and your partner stop in Two Hearts it will not help you much to make ten tricks – you will still be just scoring 60 points towards your game. You do score the extra 60 points (for making two *overtricks*), but as you had not bid them, they do not count towards game.

The score sheet at bridge looks like this:

WE	THEY

These can easily be drawn or are readily available at the stationers. Two columns, headed We and They, are each divided in two by a horizontal line. Normally all four players score and you have your own score card. At the end of the rubber it should look like a mirror image of one of your opponent's cards, with everything you have scored under WE occurring under THEY on the opponent's score sheet, and vice versa.

Points that are counting towards a game (in other words points that have been earned by bidding and making a contract) are entered *underneath* the horizontal line on the score. They are often referred to as points 'below the line'. Points that your side earn by other means (making extra tricks above your contract, or defeating a contract by the opposition) go above the line and do *not* count towards a game. They are not wasted points, for they will all add up for you at the end but they will not help you score the two games you need to win the rubber.

One thing that must have become clear by now is that it is not enough for you and your partner to choose the trump suit that suits you best – in addition you will want to decide whether you should bid a game or not. How this is best sorted out will become clear later on.

Suppose that the first three hands of a rubber have gone as

follows: on the first hand you and your partner bid and make Two
Spades with an overtrick; on the second hand your opponents bid
and make Four Hearts; and on the third hand your side bids and
makes Two Diamonds. The score will look like this:

WE	THEY
30	
60	120
40	

On the first hand you scored 60 below the line and 30 above for
the overtrick that you made but did not bid. On the second hand
the opponents scored 120 points for their game of Four Hearts. As
a result, they won the first game – just as in a tennis match, if you
had lost the first set 6–3 you would not be allowed to carry over
your three games until the next set! So when their game is scored
a line is drawn across both columns, chopping off your part-score.
When you made 40 points on the next hand, it did not make up a
game for you but started you off on the next game. You will still
need another 60 points to complete your game. At this point your
opponents have made a game and are said to be *vulnerable*; you
still have not made a game and are *not* vulnerable. This business of
vulnerability is important as you will find that it affects the penalties
incurred when a side fails to make a contract.

Now the whole point of winning a rubber is not for the feeling of
one-up-manship that it engenders. The side that first wins two
games scores a substantial bonus. If they have won the rubber by
two games to nil, they collect an additional 700 points; if they have

won by two games to one, they have an extra 500 points to come. At the end of the rubber, you add up everything (both above and below the line) in your column and subtract everything (both above and below the line) in your opponents' column. If you have scored a total of 930 points, including your bonus for winning the rubber, and the opposition have collected 190 points, you have won by a total of 740 – a win of 7 points to you as points are calculated to the nearest 100. And if you had agreed to play for 1p per hundred, you would proudly collect 7p from one of your opponents while the other one paid your partner the same amount.

The only *important* omission made so far in this summary is the scoring in no-trump contracts. This is a tiny bid odd. Basically you score the same for no-trumps as you do for a trick in a major suit contract, that is 30 points for each trick. But the first trick in any no-trump contract scores not 30, but 40 points. So 1NT (if made) would give you 40 points, 2NT 70 points, and 3NT 100 points. It is worth noting that this gives you a game, whereas to make game in spades or hearts you need to bid Four to score 120 points. In the minor suits the position is even worse, for you need to bid Five to reach the magic 100 points.

If the above is all that you ever learn about scoring, you will still have the chance to go far. The important thing to bear in mind is that you need 100 points to make a game, and it is vital to keep an eye on whether your side have got a part-score or not. Nothing is more infuriating than to have your partner raise you to Four Spades instead of leaving you in Two Spades if you only wanted another 40 points for game, particularly if you come to only nine tricks! This is why it pays for every player to keep his own score, even if it means just copying it down from the sheet of a more experienced player. It is a habit that is well worth cultivating.

At this stage this is really all you need to know about the scoring. But for completeness the assorted tables of bonuses and penalties follow. Whatever you do, don't try to memorise them. Just refer to them when necessary!

Penalties for Undertricks

Non-vulnerable	50 points per trick
Non-vulnerable, doubled	100 points for the first trick

	200 points for each subsequent trick
Non-vulnerable, redoubled	200 points for the first trick
	400 points for each subsequent trick
Vulnerable	100 points per trick
Vulnerable, doubled	200 points for the first trick
	300 points for each subsequent trick
Vulnerable, redoubled	400 points for the first trick
	600 points for each subsequent trick

Bonuses for Overtricks

Non-vulnerable	20 points in ♦ or ♣ ; 30 in ♠, ♥ or NT
Non-vulnerable, doubled	100 points per trick
Non-vulnerable, redoubled	200 points per trick
Vulnerable	20 points in ♦ or ♣ ; 30 in ♠, ♥ or NT
Vulnerable, doubled	200 points per trick
Vulnerable, redoubled	400 points per trick

Bonuses for Slams

Non-vulnerable, small slam (12 tricks)	500 points
Non-vulnerable, grand slam (13 tricks)	1000 points
Vulnerable, small slam	750 points
Vulnerable, grand slam	1500 points

Bonus for any Doubled (or Redoubled) Contract Made   50 points

Honours

For holding any four of the top five cards in the trump suit in one hand	100 points
For holding all five top honours in the trump suit in one hand	150 points
For holding all four Aces in a contract played in no-trumps in one hand	150 points

3.   Opening the bidding

So far all that has been done is to suggest that if a player has an attractive looking hand in terms of high cards, he should open the bidding with a call of One of his longest suit. However, it is quiet clear that some more rigid yardstick is needed to decide whether a hand qualifies for an opening bid. One of the commonest, and best, ways of valuing a hand is by means of the *point count*. Beware – these points have nothing to do with the points used in scoring! The point count of a hand is made up of two parts: the honour points, representing the high cards, and the distribution points catering for the possession of a long suit (clearly an asset if you can make the long suit trumps).

You count as follows:

Honour Points

For every Ace	4 points
For every King	3 points
For every Queen	2 points
For every Jack	1 point

Distribution Points

Each card more than four in any suit   1 point

Try valuing a few hands:

a	*b*	*c*
♠ A K	♠ A 3	♠ 9 5 4
♥ A K Q J 10	♥ K J 8	♥ 8 7 6
♦ A K Q	♦ A Q 9 6 2	♦ 7 5 2
♣ A K Q	♣ 8 7 4	♣ 9 5 3 2

You may think that it does not require a sophisticated point count to tell you that *a* is a more promising hand than *c*! Never mind, work out the points. Hand *a* has got four Aces (16 points), four Kings (12 points), three Queens (6 points), and one Jack (1 point). A total of 35 points. Have you forgotten anything? Yes, one distribution point for the five-card heart suit; so the hand contains 36 points.

Hand *b* has got 14 points in high cards and one distribution point for the five card diamond suit – a total of 15 points. Hand *c* by contrast is singularly depressing; no honour points and no distribution points for a gloomy total of no points at all.

It is worth noting that in each suit there are 10 points (one Ace, one King, one Queen, and one Jack). So in a complete pack of cards there are 40 honour points. But there are four players at the table, so an *average* hand contains 10 points. And if you have a hand that is only average, you have no reason to suppose that your side can make more tricks than the opposition. And remember, everything starts at six tricks, both bidding and scoring. Before you and your partner can make *any* contract, you have to come to at least seven tricks – more than your opponents. The six tricks that you have to make before anything starts are often referred to as the 'book'.

Before you open the bidding for your side you should have an above average hand. And the generally accepted standard is that you should have at least 13 points. Of course, this is not one of the *laws* of the game, but experience has shown that 13 points is a sensible standard to stick to for your minimum opening. What is more, for those who reckon these things, there is a logical reason for choosing 13 (nothing to do with superstition!).

Literally years and years of trial and error have suggested that if a partnership:

a. Hold 22 points between them they expect to make about 7 tricks.

b. Hold 24 points between them they expect to make about 8 tricks.

c. Hold 26 points between them they expect to make about 9 tricks.

d. Hold 26–28 points between them they expect to make about 10 tricks in a suit contract.

e. Hold 28–29 points between them they expect to make about 11 tricks in a suit contract.

Now if you are dealt 13 points, there are 27 to be shared among the other three hands. On average, you will find your partner with 9, and that will mean that your side will have 22 points or enough to make seven tricks. Of course, if you have started with more than 13 points you will be on even firmer ground.

Now, if you start the bidding with a call of One of a suit, this does not mean that you have *exactly* 13 points. In fact you could hold anything between 13 and 19 points and still not start with anything more exciting than one of a suit.

It is worth mentioning at this point that some of you may have been put off learning to play bridge in the past because of vague talk about a multiplicity of 'conventions' and 'systems'. Well, you can forget all about that. To be sure, some groundwork of a system is essential, else how can you and your partner know when to stop bidding and when to go on? A bidding system is simply a way of enabling you and your partner to reach a sensible contract on any pair of hands that you are dealt. If you care to think of it in this light, you have just learnt your first convention – that an opening bid of One of a suit promises at least 13 total points and probably denies more than 19.

However, a bid of a suit promises a little more than that. It tells your partner that you have what is called a *biddable* suit, that is a suit of a certain strength.

A biddable suit is one that contains at least four cards and includes at least one of the Ace, King or Queen. But a fifth card in the suit instead of one of the honours is enough to make it biddable.

A suit that you can bid again, in spite of receiving no support from your partner, is termed a *rebiddable* suit; for that you need a suit of at least five cards.

Logically enough, when you name a suit that you are suggesting as a possible trump suit, you want it to be one in which you have a certain amount of control. You do not want the opponents to be able to draw all your trumps! And either a high card or a certain amount of length gives you this measure of control.

The requirements for opening the bidding with one of a suit are threefold. You need:

1. 13–19 total points.
2. At least one biddable suit.
3. A satisfactory rebid, whatever partner responds.

It looks a little complicated, but you will be surprised how soon checking over your requirements before opening becomes second nature to you – like opening a door before walking through it! The third condition is new, but it is perhaps the most important. It is on this, more than any other, that a successful auction hinges. It means, quite simply, that if you open the bidding with one of a suit and your partner replies with a bid in *another* suit, you must be prepared to make at least one more bid. If you have a rebiddable suit, or good support for your partner's suit, it is easy. But, before you rush to open the bidding, you must be prepared to bid again, *whatever your partner responds.*

So if you had been dealt:

♠ A K J 5 2
♥ K Q 7
♦ 5 4
♣ J 9 2

you would have no problem. You have 14 honour points and one distributional point for the fifth spade. Your spades are perfectly rebiddable, so you can start off quite happily with One Spade, secure in the knowledge that you can bid the spades again on the second round if partner bids something that does not appeal to you, like Two Diamonds.

However, you will often be dealt hands with more than one biddable suit and your choice for the opening bid will be critical. There are really five basic rules that cover the vast majority of situations. They are:

1. With two biddable or rebiddable suits of unequal length, bid the longer.

2. With three biddable four-card suits, bid the suit *ranking below* the singleton.

3. With two *touching* biddable four-card suits, bid the higher ranking suit. (By touching suits we mean spades and hearts, or hearts and diamonds, or diamonds and clubs – suits next door to one another in the ranking order.)

4. With two non-touching biddable four-card suits, bid the lower ranking.

5. With two rebiddable suits of equal length, bid the higher ranking.

There are a variety of theoretical reasons for these rules or guidelines, some quite deep and so way beyond an introduction to the game. Although you will appreciate the backing reasons later on in your bridge career, for the time being you will do well simply to follow them unquestioningly. Perhaps one example would be worthwhile – suppose you were dealt:

♠ A K 7 4
♥ 8 6 3
♦ 4 2
♣ A K 7 4

This is clearly a case for rule 4 – two non-touching biddable four-card suits – and the recommended advice is to open with one of the lower-ranking suit, that is begin with One Club. Suppose you disregarded this advice and started with One Spade. If your partner responds Two Diamonds you will have to make another bid (remember your promise when you opened the bidding – to make a rebid if partner responded in a new suit) and your spades are not rebiddable. There is not much left but Three Clubs and already you have carried the bidding up to the Three level with no assurance of a trump suit satisfactory to both partners. But think what would have happened if you had dutifully opened One Club – partner could tell you about his diamond suit by bidding One Diamond, and you could mention your spades with One Spade. Result – just as much information conveyed to partner without taking the bidding up beyond the One level.

All well and good so far, but every once in a while you will pick up a hand like this:

♠ J 9 6 3
♥ A J 4
♦ K Q 7
♣ K 9 8

Do you see the problem? You have 14 points – quite enough for an opening bid, but you have no biddable suit, let alone a convenient rebid! Now this situation usually only arises when you have been dealt what is called a *balanced hand* – a hand with no void, no singleton and no two doubletons; a hand with a shape of 4–3–3–3 or 4–4–3–2 or 5–3–3–2.

The solution is surprisingly simple. If the five card suit is not a major, you open these hands with a bid of One No-trumps. Now, strictly speaking this is a weak no-trump – you may at some time in the future hear bridge players talk about playing the strong no-trump. However, to keep things simple we are going to stick to the weak no-trump for our bidding. This means that every time you or your partner open the bidding with 1NT you are *guaranteeing* a balanced hand of the type discussed above, with 13 or 14 points. No less, or you would have passed; no more for then you would have had to look elsewhere for your opening bid. The opening bid of 1NT as we shall use it is a very precise weapon, telling partner to within a point how strong your hand is.

It is worth while digressing from the subject of opening bids for a moment to consider how partner should react when he hears you open with a bid of 1NT. Later on we will be dealing with the situation in which the responder positively hates the idea of no-trumps, but suppose he has a balanced hand, like the opener's, with no long suits and no short suits. Clearly there is no need for him to bid anything but no-trumps. The whole problem reduces to one of simple arithmetic! You have already learnt that a combined holding of 26 points should be enough to produce nine tricks. And there you have it – if you *know* for certain that your partner has 13 or 14 points and you can see how many you have in your own hand, it is not difficult to judge whether you can make 3NT or not. And 3NT represents a game!

If you like the idea of no-trumps you simply pass with 11 points or less – you know that as a partnership you fall short of the required 26 points. With 13 points or more, there is no need to hold back. Over partner's bid of 1NT you raise directly to 3NT. It is only when you have exactly 12 points in your responding hand that you cannot be quite sure. However, it is not an insoluble problem. You raise to 2NT, inviting your partner to go on to 3NT if he has started with a maximum holding of 14 points and warning him that he would be better advised to pass if he has started with a minimum of 13 points.

Once you have opened 1NT you have no further problems! If partner raises to 3NT you are quite content for you are in game; if he passes you will not have another chance to speak. It is only when he raises to 2NT that you have a final decision to take; and, as we have seen, this is not a difficult one if you can count how many points you have.

Incidentally, you can see why it is just as bad to have too many points for an opening of 1NT as it is to have too few; just suppose that you had opened 1NT with 16 points, arguing that the odd Queen extra could hardly make any real difference. It might well do so if partner has started with 11 points – as he 'knows' that you cannot hold more than 14 points he will pass, and what might have been an easy game will have slipped you by. No-trump bidding is, of necessity, very precise.

4.   Suit establishment and entries

When you play a hand as declarer it is extremely rare that a sight of dummy shows that you have enough immediate winners for your contract. Far more often there will be the need to *establish* tricks, in other words to get cards other than Aces and Kings working for you. There are three basic ways of going about this problem, but one of them, finessing, warrants a whole chapter to itself later on.

However, let's take the simplest possibility first. Suppose you have a suit such as **K Q** in one hand and two low cards (usually designated as xx, if they are unimportant small cards). There are no instant tricks that you can take for the opponents hold the Ace. But you are in a position to *establish* a trick very easily in this suit. All you have to do is lead it and force an opponent to win with his Ace. Then your remaining high card is a trick that can be cashed or taken whenever you like. There are a host of examples in this vein – in each one of the following cases tricks will eventually come in if you can lead the suit enough times. How many tricks should you come to with:

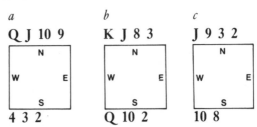

a	b	c
Q J 10 9	**K J 8 3**	**J 9 3 2**
4 3 2	**Q 10 2**	**10 8**

Yes, you are quite right: two, three and one respectively, losing in *a* two tricks to the Ace and King, in *b* one trick to the Ace and in *c* three tricks to the Ace, King and Queen. There are a couple of traps to watch out for – if you had started with **Q 10 3** facing **J 4 2** it would do you no good to lead the 3 from one hand and play the 2 from the other. That will not force out either of the opponents' high cards – they will win the trick peacefully with the 6 or 7 and still have the Ace and King left. It is essential to play a high card from one hand or the other – then, when the Ace and King have been driven out you will be left with one high card that will be worth a trick.

Equally, if you had started with **J 4 2** facing **Q 5 3** you would not have enough material to force a trick – your Queen could lose to the King, your Jack to the Ace and you won't come to any tricks with what is left! But provided that you have enough high cards to force out all the higher missing cards and still leave yourself with something worthwhile at the end, this technique can often be used to bring in tricks.

The other possibility is to get your low cards to work for you. It sounds unlikely, but if you have enough cards in the suit it can be surprisingly effective. Take a simple case:

A K Q 2

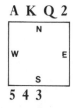

5 4 3

Here you have three obvious tricks, but there is a distinct chance that the 2 can become a trick as well. Do you see what you need to happen? This is a suit in which you have started with seven cards, leaving six for the opponents. Now, if these missing six cards are divided three-three between the opposition partners you are in the money. Playing off the Ace, King and Queen will remove *all* of their cards and leave your 2 as the last card in the suit and a trick. Of course this is no certainty; more often than a 3–3 break you will find the missing cards divided 4–2 or worse, and nothing extra will come in. *The more cards that you and your partner have to start with in a suit, the better your chances of getting the low cards to work for you.* And if you have started with fewer cards in the suit than the other side, you have virtually no chance of getting your low cards to help. If you hold:

```
            A K Q 2
          ┌─────────┐
          │    N    │
          │ W     E │
          │    S    │
          └─────────┘
            4 3
```

then your side has only six cards in the suit. No matter how the remaining seven were shared between the opponents, someone would be left with something to beat the 2 after you had played off the three top honours.

The idea of using a long suit in this fashion is well illustrated with the following example:

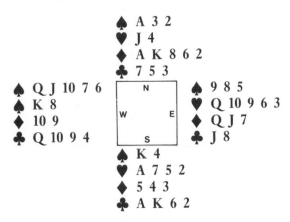

Suppose that South is declarer in 3NT and that West leads the Queen of spades. Inspection of dummy shows declarer that there are seven top winners in the Ace and King of spades, the Ace of hearts, the Ace and King of diamonds and the Ace and King of clubs. Clearly two tricks have got to be established from somewhere. Bearing in mind that it is only suits in which declarer and dummy combined hold more cards than the defenders that hold promise of extra tricks from low cards, South can immediately reject both spades and hearts as a source of extra tricks. Of the remaining two suits, although declarer's side holds a majority in both, it is the diamonds that look more promising for there are eight cards in the combined hands compared with seven in clubs. Furthermore, even with an even break in clubs, only *one* extra trick would come in and that would not be enough. However, with diamonds there are only five cards missing and the big hope is that these cards are divided 3-2 between the opponents. The suit can then be established by cashing the Ace and King (thus drawing four of the missing five cards in diamonds as both opponents have to follow suit), then leading another round, conceding a trick to the outstanding high card. Once that is done, the last two diamonds in dummy will be established as tricks as no one else will have any cards left in the suit.

That's fine; you have formed a plan that will yield the two necessary extra tricks if the suit breaks kindly. But there is a more immediate problem with which to deal. The opening lead against you was the Queen of spades. Now, do you see what will happen if you win with the Ace of spades in dummy and clear the diamond suit as suggested? You will certainly end with two winning diamonds on the table, but to your horror you will find *that there is no possible way to get the lead to dummy to make these winners.*

Could you have done anything about this? Yes, by planning a little in advance. If you had taken the precaution of winning the opening lead with the King of spades in your hand, you would still have the Ace in dummy as a vital *entry* to get to the winning diamonds.

It is no good *establishing* winners if you don't have the necessary entries to the hand to *cash* the winners.

There is another point worth noting about the hand. You have seen that declarer's best play was to attack the suit in which he and his partner held the most cards. The same applies to the defenders against a no-trump contract. It is rare for them to have enough top winners to defeat the contract out of hand – their best chance of developing enough tricks for their purpose is to lead, and continue to lead, their longest suit in the hope of establishing it and getting their low cards to work. You will get nowhere in defence if you just cash a few Aces and hope for the best.

The declarer's problem could have been made more difficult. Suppose that these were the two hands:

♠ 4 3 2
♥ J 4
♦ A K 8 6 2
♣ 7 5 3

♠ A K
♥ A 7 5 2
♦ 5 4 3
♣ A K 6 2

Do you see what has happened? The Ace of spades has migrated from the North hand to the South. If the contract and opening lead are the same as before declarer will have to plan things anew before he starts to play, for now there is no possibility of an outside entry to dummy reaching the winning diamonds. Just think what happened last time you played the hand – you made two tricks in diamonds, then gave one away, then made two more. In other words you could not make the two extra tricks until you had conceded one to the opposition. That should give a clue: after winning the opening spade lead in hand you should lead a diamond and simply play low from dummy, immediately giving the opponents the trick that they are bound to come to. Once a round of diamonds has been played (provided that the suit is breaking 3–2) there will be only three missing and these will be divided between the two opponents. So on regaining the lead declarer can play off the Ace and King of diamonds to leave the last two diamonds as winners. And the key is that he still has the lead in dummy to make these much needed extra tricks.

Digressing for the moment, you may think that it is an easy matter to be able to cash tricks once they have been established. Well, this is not always so. You have already met one situation in which winners can be left stranded in a hand with no possible entry. And there is no sadder sight in bridge than that – winners left high and dry like whales on a beach. But there is another position in which it is easy to go wrong. Suppose that you have started with three ready set-up winners in a suit like this:

A Q 3

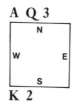

K 2

Now, what could be easier than cashing these winners? Nothing, as long as you set about it the right way. Just suppose that you started by leading the 2 and won the trick with the Ace or Queen. You would be forced to take the next trick with the King. And then? Oh dear, there is a high card in one hand, just waiting to be cashed, but the lead is in the *other* hand. Sometimes Providence arranges for you to have another entry in some other suit so that you can recover from your slip. But not always. And yet there was no need to get into trouble. As long as you had won the first trick with the King you would have had a low card to lead across and make the Ace, followed by the Queen. To jam up a suit at the very beginning in the way suggested is known as *blocking* the suit and is clearly something to be avoided if at all possible. The secret when playing a suit of this type is to *play off the high cards first from the hand with the shorter holding* (that is, the hand with the fewer cards).

You should follow this principle even when you are establishing a suit. Take this example:

Q J 10 9 5

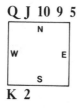

K 2

To establish the suit you should lead the King first – the high card from the shorter hand. Just see what might happen if you go wrong: suppose that you are in a no-trump contract and require five of the last six tricks. Only spades and diamonds are left, and the Ace of spades is still missing.

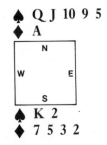

♠ Q J 10 9 5
♦ A

♠ K 2
♦ 7 5 3 2

It is clear that the Ace of spades has to be knocked out, but suppose that South breaks the rules and leads ♠2 from his hand. The opponents win with ♠A and play back a diamond to dummy's Ace. Now the next spade lead has to be won in declarer's hand and to his fury he has to concede the last three tricks to whatever diamonds the opponents have left. However, if declarer had started by leading ♠K from his hand, nothing could have gone wrong – dummy would have been able to make the remaining tricks after ♠A had been driven out.

Although you don't have to be anything of a mathematician to play bridge (some of the best players I've known have found it difficult to give the right change for 2p), it can often be a help to have some idea of whether a suit is likely to break favourably for you or not.

Take the diamond suit from the two hands examined earlier:

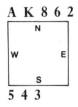

A K 8 6 2

5 4 3

You will remember that the contract hinged on finding the missing five diamonds divided 3–2 between the opponents. This is often spoken of as a '3–2 break', and as 3–2 was the best possible break from declarer's point of view, you would talk of the suit 'breaking favourably'. However, if one opponent had held all five and his partner none they would have 'broken unfavourably' – in fact, very unfavourably indeed! – and put paid to any real chance of making 3NT.

There is a rather curious rule that tells you what the most probable break is for any number of cards. *If you are missing an odd number of cards, the most probable division is the one nearest to even.* So with seven cards missing the most likely break is 4–3; with five cards missing 3–2 and so on. *With an even number of cards missing, the most probable division is the one nearest to even that is not precisely even.* With six cards missing, although you might hope for a 3–3 break, the most likely division is 4–2. Be careful, this guide only suggests *probabilities*. Please don't write to tell me that six missing cards divided 3–3. Most of the time they will not.

Just to show you that the ideas of counting tricks and (if necessary) not blocking suits also occur in suit play as well as no-trumps, consider this deal:

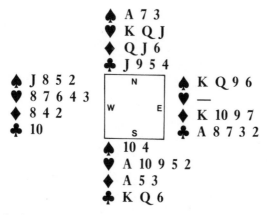

North dealt the cards, and with 14 points and a balanced hand had no difficulty in selecting 1NT as his opening bid. However, South with his fair heart suit was not keen on the idea of no-trumps and the final contract was Four Hearts played by South. West led his singleton 10 of clubs, hoping to get some ruffs with his small trumps. Declarer played low from dummy and East won with ♣A. Already declarer had a critical play to make. With the ten of clubs out of the way, the King, Queen, Jack and 9 were all equal and if he had followed suit with the 6 the remainder of the suit would have been blocked. It cost nothing to unblock in order to keep the club suit fluid, and declarer passed the test with flying colours when he dropped ♣Q under the Ace. A club came back and South continued the good work by playing the King. To his annoyance West trumped and led a spade. Declarer won with dummy's Ace and was able to draw all four of the outstanding trumps before any more damage could be done. Then, as a result of his foresight in unblocking the clubs, he was able to cross to dummy with ♣9 and cash ♣J to discard his losing spade. All that had to be done now was to lead diamonds and give up a trick to the King in order to establish a trick for one of dummy's diamond honours and declarer had ten tricks for his contract.

Do you see what would have happened if declarer had not unblocked in clubs? The play would have gone in the same way except that there would have been no possible entry to the table to make ♣J – remember, it cannot be cashed while West still has any trumps. Although declarer could eventually get the lead to dummy with one of the diamond honours it would only be after losing a trick to ♦K, and when East was in with ♦K he would be in a position to cash a spade trick. That would have been the fourth trick for the defence and would have spelt defeat for declarer.

5.   Limit bids as responder

If your partner opens the bidding with One of a suit, you do not,
as yet, know a great deal about his hand. True, you know that he
has at least 13 points and that he is unlikely to hold more than 19
(for then he would have looked for a more exciting opening bid).
You also know that he has named his longest suit, or at least that he
has no longer suit. However, that still leaves a tremendous range of
possibilities. Apart from not being sure of his strength, you do not
know whether he has a one-suited, two-suited or three-suited hand
and it is always possible that he has a balanced hand suited to no-
trumps but with the wrong number of points to open 1NT. All in
all, it is rare that you, as responder, can make an immediate decision
as to what the best final contract should be. As a result, most of the
time you will make a reply that starts to describe your hand.

TYPES OF REPLY

There are four different types of reply that you can make to an
opening bid in a suit by partner:

1. Say No Bid.
2. Support partner's suit.
3. Respond in no-trumps.
4. Bid a new suit.

The fourth of these possibilities is a big topic and, having listed
it with the others for completeness, we will leave it until the next
chapter.

We can also dismiss the first quite quickly. As you know that the
opening bidder does not hold more than 20 points and that 26 are
needed before there will be a sensible chance of making a game,
there is a simple guide-line – *with fewer than 6 points you should
pass an opening bid of one of a suit from your partner.* As in other

walks of life, the road for bridge players is full of temptations. Suppose you had been dealt:

♠ 10 8 6 5 4 3
♥ —
♦ J 9 7 6 3
♣ 8 4

and heard partner open One Heart. Your natural instinct is to respond One Spade, arguing that anything would be better than One Heart. You might fall on your feet if partner is able to support spades or even bid diamonds, but in practice he never seems to oblige. Instead he rebids his hearts and there you are – at least one level higher and with nothing to show for your pains. No, even allowing for your long suits, you have only 4 points and should simply pass the opening bid. It is most unlikely that your side can make a game and, while One Heart may not be the ideal contract, at least you will have avoided a major disaster. It could well be that the opponents intervene and that there will be some more bidding; possibly you will have a chance to show your Spades later, but at least you will have told partner categorically that you lack 6 pts to respond: he won't get too excited if we subsequently bid our Spades.

The remaining two types of response that you can make have a lot in common and are called *limit bids* for a reason that will soon appear.

SUPPORTING PARTNER'S SUIT

Normally, before you support partner, you need at least four cards in his suit. This makes good sense if you think of it in this light: partner's bid only guarantees four cards in the suit he has named. He *may* have more, but you can only rely on four. If you support him with only 3 trumps, you could easily end up in a high level contract with only 7 trumps between the hands, leaving 6 for the opponents. Now a majority of 7 against 6 is not a very healthy state of affairs. Suppose the opponents lead something that you are forced to ruff, perhaps twice. Then you would be in a position where your side was left with fewer trumps than the other side and your reason for choosing that suit as trumps would have gone out of the window. However, if your side had started with one more trump, that is 8, that would mean one less for the opposition. A majority of 8 against 5 is a much more satisfactory proposition than 7 against 6. Even after ruffing twice you still retain the upper hand.

Another important point about supporting partner is that you should not worry about the *strength* of your trump support: when you are looking for a good trump suit it is the *number of cards* you hold that matters.

Suppose that you had been dealt this hand:

♠ A 5 3
♥ 10 6 4 2
♦ Q 8 7 4
♣ J 5

and heard partner open One Heart. Clearly with 7 points you are worth a bid and you have four-card support for partner's hearts. On the other hand, you could not describe this as an exciting collection of cards and you would not want to do anything too ambitious. It is sufficient to raise to Two Hearts. This tells your partner that you like his hearts and that *your hand contains 6–9 points*.

It could be that you had started with a slightly stronger hand:

♠ A 5 3
♥ 10 6 4 2
♦ A Q 8 7
♣ J 5

You are, in fact, an Ace stronger than in the previous example – a whole trick better off. And yet if partner has only a minimum 13 points for his opening bid the partnership will still be just short of the required 26 points that it needs for game. The solution is to raise partner's bid to Three Hearts. This tells your partner that you like his hearts and that *your hand contains 10–12 points*. In spite of the encouraging sound of this bid, it does not compel partner to speak again. The message is that, if partner has a minimum opening bid with 13 points, you expect to make 9 tricks with hearts as trumps. If, of course, he has *more* than the 13 points that he has already promised, then you will be delighted to hear him go on to Four Hearts.

Again, you might have started with an even stronger hand.

Suppose we step up the last deal by adding another trick – the King of spades:

♠ A K 5
♥ 10 6 4 2
♦ A Q 8 7
♣ J 5

Now, with 14 points, you don't mind how weak partner's opening bid may be – he has at least 13 points and you know that your partnership holds at least 27 points. Hence you want to be in game and the bid is Four Hearts. This tells your partner that you like his hearts and that *your hand contains 13–15 points.*

You can see why these bids are called limit bids – when you support partner's suit you always do so to the full limit of your hand, and as a result your partner knows the strength of your hand to within a point or two. Although you don't know how strong your partner is, he knows practically everything about your hand and can make an intelligent decision as to whether the partnership should be in game or not.

ADDITIONAL POINTS

The description above gives the skeleton structure of limit raises in partner's suit, but it doesn't take quite everything into account. Imagine that partner has opened One Spade and that you hold in succession:

a	b
♠ Q 9 7 4	♠ Q 9 7 4
♥ A 8 5	♥ A 8 5 2
♦ K 7 3	♦ K 7 3 2
♣ 9 6 4	♣ 9

The point-count suggests that both of these hands are equal in value, with 9 points, and are both worth a raise to Two Spades. But suppose partner has opened with:

♠ A K J 5
♥ K Q 3
♦ Q J 5
♣ 8 7 2

With 16 points and the knowledge that partner holds spade support and 6–9 points there is no incentive for him to go on, for the absolute maximum that the partnership can hold is 25 points and that will not be enough for game. With hand *a* everything goes according to plan – the defenders have three clubs and a diamond to take immediately. However, if responder holds hand *b* then ten tricks, if not eleven, should be easy. There are, after all, only two quick losers. The additional strength of hand *b* lies not in the fact that it has one more diamond and one more heart than hand *a* but in the *singleton* club. And it would have been even better if there had been a void in clubs instead of the singleton!

Most players are familiar with the idea of adding distributional points for long suits if they are thinking of opening the bidding, but when you are supporting your partner's suit the factor that improves your hand is having a shortage or shortages elsewhere in the hand. Expressing this in terms of points, we have:

When supporting partner's suit add 3 points for a void.
When supporting partner's suit add 2 points for a singleton.
When supporting partner's suit add 1 point for a doubleton.

In general, long suits are not taken into consideration when supporting partner, but there is one exception to this. If you hold extra length in the suit you are raising, you may add one point for each card over four. So if partner opened One Heart and you held:

♠ A
♥ K 8 5 4 2
♦ K 7 5
♣ 9 5 4 2

you would value your hand as 10 points in high cards, 2 points for the singleton spade, and 1 point for the fifth card in partner's suit. That gives you 13 points *in support of hearts*, and your response to One Heart should be Four Hearts.

Don't fall into the trap of imagining that shortages are in any way useful when you are thinking of opening the bidding. A void, say, in these circumstances is a very doubtful asset indeed. It may be in the suit that your partner insists on making trumps! Then it would be a positive disadvantage. I can always remember a pupil regarding this hand:

♠ K 7 6 5 3 2
♥ Q 7
♦ —
♣ J 8 7 6 2

He argued that he held 6 points in high cards, 2 points for a six-card suit, 1 point for a five-card suit, 3 points for a void and 2 points for a doubleton – 13 points in all! Needless to say, the hand does not begin to be an opening bid.

In the same way that the responder's hand improves when he is prepared to support his partner, so does the opener's hand when his suit is supported. Suppose that you have opened the bidding with One Heart on:

♠ K 7 4 2
♥ K Q J 7 3
♦ A 9 6
♣ 4

and your partner raises to Three Hearts. You have 13 points in high cards and 1 point for your five-card suit. But as soon as your partner supports hearts, you can revalue your hand and take the singleton club into account, giving you two more points – a total of 16 points. Partner, you know, has 10–12 points and the partnership must have at least 26 points between them. So you would go on to Four Hearts. Even if partner has a complete minimum there should be a fair play for game. Suppose the two hands were:

a	*b*
♠ K 7 4 2	♠ A 8
♥ K Q J 7 3	♥ 10 9 5 2
♦ A 9 6	♦ K Q 8
♣ 4	♣ 9 6 5 2

The responder has only 9 high card points, but he adds 1 for his doubleton spade – just enough for the limit raise to Three Hearts. It is true that these hands 'fit' very well; there are no losers in spades or diamonds, and the partnership might easily make eleven tricks, losing only one club and the Ace of trumps.

One point about limit raises cannot be stressed too strongly. If you hold four or more cards of a major suit in which your partner has opened the bidding and can, as a result, make a limit raise, then there is no virtue in doing anything else. Indeed, it can be a mistake. Suppose you were dealt:

♠ A K Q 4
♥ 10 8 7 3
♦ J 4 2
♣ 8 7

and heard One Heart from partner. Go on, admit it. You would be tempted to tell him about your spades. However, that would be misguided: if you do start by responding One Spade you will never convince partner that you have got four of his hearts. The bidding may wind on and on to end up in the wrong contract. Correct (and much simpler) is a limit raise to Three Hearts, telling partner that you hold at least four cards in his suit and 10–12 points. As you can see, in support of hearts you have 11 points (don't forget 1 for the doubleton club). Don't feel that you have to 'show' partner your spades, the time to do that is when you put dummy down! After all, you can make only one suit trumps and you have already found a perfectly satisfactory suit in which the partnership must hold at least eight cards.

SUPPORTING PARTNER'S MINOR SUIT

You may wonder why emphasis has been laid on supporting partner's *major* suit. What if partner has started with One of a minor suit (clubs or diamonds)? Does this affect your response if you have support for his suit? Not a great deal, but there is one thought that you ought to keep in mind. To make game in a minor suit means taking eleven tricks. Now a good trump suit that both partners like is usually worth at least one trick in the play. If a partnership with a good fit in, say, spades has a choice between playing in Four Spades or 3NT the suit contract will on balance be best. But even with a good fit in a minor suit it may (unless the hands are very distributional) be better to play for nine tricks in no-trumps rather than eleven in the minor suit. As a result, limit raises in clubs and diamonds are affected in two ways.

1 If you have a biddable major suit, it will be as well to show this first rather than raise partner's minor suit to Two or Three. He may have support for the suit you bid, or it may enable him to suggest no-trumps as an alternative contract.

2 If you have the values to raise to the Four level (13–15 points), you must remember that neither Four Clubs or Four Diamonds will give you game. With a hand of this strength you will do better to show another suit first or even suppress your support in order to bid no-trumps with a suitable hand.

So with:

♠ A 8 4
♥ 8 3
♦ K 10 5
♣ K 8 6 4 3

you simply raise One Club to Three Clubs. But with:

♠ A 10 8 4
♥ 8 3
♦ K 10 5
♣ K 8 6 4

you would be better advised to try One Spade rather than Three Clubs. (The implications of responding in a new suit will be discussed in the next chapter). Again, if partner opens One Diamond and you hold:

♠ K 5
♥ 8 7
♦ A J 8 3
♣ A 10 9 7 3

it is better to 'mark-time' with a bid of Two Clubs than go for the limit raise to Four Diamonds which your hand is worth.

RESPONDING IN NO-TRUMPS

Immediate responses in no-trumps are made when the opener's partner has *a balanced hand without four cards support for the opening bid.* Just as an opening bid of 1NT suggests no long suits, no short suits and high cards well shared out over the suits, so does any reply in no-trumps to a suit opening. Just as when raising partner's suit you follow the principle that the more you have got, the more you bid, so you do when responding in no-trumps. As with raises of partner's suit, responses in no-trumps are *limit bids*.

Suppose partner opens with One Heart and you hold:

♠ K 7 4
♥ J 8
♦ Q 8 6 5
♣ Q 9 8 2

No short suits (the slight weakness in hearts is covered by partner's opening bid), no particularly long suits about which you feel you have to tell partner, high cards well distributed over the hand. All in all, a perfect hand on which to respond in no-trumps. With only 8 points there is no chance of a game unless partner is very strong, but it is necessary to keep the bidding alive in case he has got 18 points or more in which case you do want to end in game. The response of 1NT is ideal; just like the single raise of partner's suit it shows 6–9 points. Note that when you respond in no-trumps you cannot add a distributional point for the doubleton in hearts – even if it was not in partner's suit, a shortage would be of no possible use in a no-trump contract.

If the responder had started with a slightly stronger hand, say:

♠ K 7 4
♥ A 8
♦ Q 8 6 5
♣ Q 9 8 2

the response would be 2NT, showing a balanced hand with 10–12 points. Like the double raise in partner's suit (showing the same sort of strength) this is not forcing. In other words, partner will only go on if he has something to spare in addition to the 13 points he has already promised by opening the bidding.

With an even stronger holding:

♠ K J 4
♥ A 8
♦ K J 8 6
♣ Q 9 8 2

the responder goes straight to 3NT, suggesting a balanced hand with 13–15 points. Now he does not mind how weak the opening bid is, as he knows that there are at least 26 points between the two hands and game will be a good proposition.

It is worth considering what action the opening bidder should take after hearing a limit bid in no-trumps from his partner. If he is happy with the suggestion of no-trumps there will be no reason for him to go back to a suit. It will simply be a question of deciding whether the partnership has enough for game or not. Say the opening bid of One Heart was based on this hand:

♠ A 9 5

♥ K Q 9 7 5

♦ A 9

♣ J 10 3

With honours in all four suits and no voids or singletons the opener is quite content with the idea of no-trumps. If the reply had been 1NT (6–9 points) he can judge that there are not enough points to make game worthwhile and will simply pass. If the reply had been 2NT (10–12 points) then the opening bidder's 15 points (remember 1 point for the fifth heart) make a raise to 3NT an attractive bet. And finally if the response had been 3NT there would be no reason to disturb this contract.

However, the opening bidder may have a hand that is quite unsuited to partner's suggestion of no-trumps. He may hold:

♠ A 10 4

♥ K Q 10 9 7 5

♦ —

♣ A 5 4 2

Taking the six-card suit into account, he has 15 points. This will not be enough for game facing a known 6–9 points, and the opening bidder will do better to convert back to Two Hearts after a response of 1NT. Suppose however that the response was 2NT – the opening bidder must take care not to rebid Three Hearts which would merely suggest a dislike of no-trumps and insufficient values for game. Instead he should bid what he thinks he can make, namely Four Hearts. Finally, if the response had been 3NT the opener should still go back to hearts – the diamonds may be sufficiently well-guarded, but there is no need to take any risks. Partner is known to hold at least two hearts (he has, after all, promised a balanced hand) and hearts will be much safer than no-trumps.

To sum up with the aid of a table:

POINTS	6-9	10-12	13-15
With four card or better support in partner's suit	Raise to Two	Raise to Three	Raise to Four
Without four card support for a partner and a balanced hand	Respond 1NT	Respond 2NT	Respond 3NT

Remember that once you have made one of the above limit bids you can relax. You have described your hand completely, both as to the type of hand that you hold and the number of points that you have. After that it will be partner who is best equipped to judge whether or not a game is sensible. In the normal course of events (although there are some exceptions) you will not be expected to bid again once you have limited your hand.

EXAMPLES OF LIMIT RESPONSES IN ACTION

Dealer, North

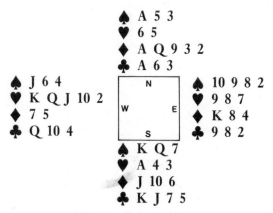

♠ A 5 3
♥ 6 5
♦ A Q 9 3 2
♣ A 6 3

♠ J 6 4   ♠ 10 9 8 2
♥ K Q J 10 2   ♥ 9 8 7
♦ 7 5   ♦ K 8 4
♣ Q 10 4   ♣ 9 8 2

♠ K Q 7
♥ A 4 3
♦ J 10 6
♣ K J 7 5

North opened One Diamond for, although he had the right number of points to open 1NT, the respectable five card suit and the weak doubleton in hearts made the suit opening preferable. After a pass by East, South held the perfect hand for a response of 3NT, guaranteeing a balanced hand and 13–15 points. The level was too high for West to take any action, and North had no reason to run away from the idea of no-trumps once partner had suggested it, so 3NT became the final contract.

With his strong heart suit West had a natural lead and chose the King (to lead the top of a sequence of touching cards is conventional). Declarer could see seven top winners that he could take without losing the lead. The most promising suit to develop was the diamonds where there was only the King missing; certainly a successful finesse in the suit would bring in enough tricks and to spare, but if the finesse lost there was the danger that East would be able to return a heart and the defenders might be able to take enough heart tricks to defeat the contract. South found a neat way to improve his chances, a way that could easily have been overlooked in the heat of the moment. He refused to take ♥K with his Ace and still held off when West continued with the Queen. He was forced to take the third round but you can see the effect of his hold-up play: when he did take the losing diamond finesse into East's hand East had been run out of hearts and was reduced to playing a harmless spade back. Now declarer had ten tricks to take and the game was safe.

Dealer, South

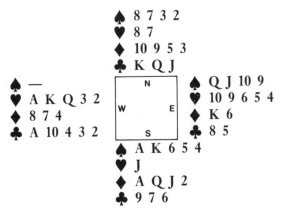

```
                    ♠ 8 7 3 2
                    ♥ 8 7
                    ♦ 10 9 5 3
                    ♣ K Q J
    ♠ —                           ♠ Q J 10 9
    ♥ A K Q 3 2     N             ♥ 10 9 6 5 4
    ♦ 8 7 4      W     E          ♦ K 6
    ♣ A 10 4 3 2    S             ♣ 8 5
                    ♠ A K 6 5 4
                    ♥ J
                    ♦ A Q J 2
                    ♣ 9 7 6
```

This was the bidding:

South	West	North	East
1♠	2♥	2♠ *a*	3♥ *b*
3♠ *c*	4♥ *d*	No	No
4♠ *e*	No	No	Dble *f*
No	No	No	

a. A limit bid in support of spades.

b. East has 9 points in support of partner's hearts; possibly the bid of Three Hearts is a little aggressive, but with both opponents bidding there is a danger of being shut out completely.

c. Once South's spades have been supported his hand improves by 2 points, but not sufficiently to try for game.

d. In the same way West's hand is improved once his hearts have been supported and with his distributional advantages it looks as though his side should have a fair play per game.

e. Once South's spades have been supported it does not look as though there will be many tricks for North–South if they defend against Four Hearts. South goes on to Four Spades, not because he is particularly hopeful of making his contract, but because he does not expect it to fail by more than one trick. Going one down is a good investment if the opponents can make game.

f. With two certain trump tricks and a partner who has done a fair amount of bidding, East's double looks a good bet.

Against Four Spades doubled West started with two rounds of hearts and South ruffed. With high hopes of making his contract declarer tried ♠A but West showed out to expose the 4–0 break. There was no point in playing any more trumps – East was bound to win two tricks in the suit no matter what South tried – so declarer turned his attention to clubs. West took his Ace and, for want of anything better to do, returned another club to dummy's Queen. Now, with the lead in dummy, declarer led ♦10 and ran it when East played low. The ten won and with the lead still on the table South played another diamond. When East's King appeared declarer knew that he had escaped for one off. He played out his remaining minor suit winners and East was welcome to his two trump tricks whenever he cared to take them. Declarer was one down doubled, losing 100 points, but this was a worthwhile save as East–West would have had no trouble in making their game call of Four Hearts.

6.

Unlimited bids as responder

In the last chapter we discussed limit responses to an opening suit call – bids that define the strength of responder's hand very precisely. On a lot of hands, however, you will find yourself in a position where you neither want to support partner's suit nor reply in no-trumps. Instead you want to tell opener about your suit. It would be very nice if you could tell him about the strength of your hand at the same time – nice, but impracticable. If partner opened One Heart and you held a good diamond suit it would be disastrous to have to bid Two Diamonds with 6–9 points, Three Diamonds with 10–12 points, and so on. Just imagine an auction starting One Heart – Four Diamonds! You would be at the Four level already without any idea of what was the best trump suit. For all you knew the right contract might be 3NT and the bidding would have gone well past that already.

UNLIMITED RESPONSES TO SUIT CALLS

There was no such difficulty when you were making one of the limit bids, for then you knew in what denomination you wanted to play the hand. But when you are bidding a new suit, the search for the right denomination in which to play the hand is still on. When you respond in a new suit to a suit opening call, therefore, you do not rush things. If partner opens One Heart you will respond One Spade with:

♠ A Q 8 6 3
♥ 5
♦ 9 7 4
♣ 10 8 6 2

But equally you will still just respond One Spade with either of these hands:

♠ A Q 8 6 3   ♠ A Q 8 6 3
♥ 5   ♥ 5
♦ A 7 4   ♦ A 7 4
♣ 10 8 6 2   ♣ A 8 6 2

There is an important consequence of this as far as the opening bidder is concerned. If he opens the bidding with One of a suit and his partner replies in a *new* suit, then the opener must speak again, for no matter how weak his opening bid it is possible that the partnership has the values for a game. Note that this only applies if the response is in a *new* suit – after a limit raise in the opener's suit or a limit response in no-trumps, or if partner has originally passed, the opener is quiet free to pass when he can judge that his side is short of game-going values.

Sometimes as responder you will have a choice between showing a new suit and making a limit bid in no-trumps. On the face of it, the limit bid would seem to be better as it tells partner just how strong your hand is – unlike the response in a new suit which, as we have seen, is unlimited. However, another factor has to be taken into account.

Consider these two hands:

         West   *East*
      ♠ A 5   ♠ K 9 6 4
      ♥ J 10 7 3   ♥ Q 9 8 6
      ♦ A K 7 6 4   ♦ 8 5
      ♣ 5 2   ♣ Q 9 4

After One Diamond from West, East can choose from One Spade, One Heart and 1NT as possible responses. Looking at both hands, it is not difficult to see that the best contract is with hearts as trumps – a suit in which there are eight cards between the two hands. Played in hearts there are only four certain losers (you must lose tricks to the Ace and King of Hearts and to the Ace and King of Clubs no matter how the play goes); played with diamonds as trumps there are the same four top losers and at least one trick in diamonds to be lost; and played in no-trumps the situation in clubs is, to say the least, somewhat delicate. How, then, can you give yourself the best chance of ending in a heart contract? If East's original response to One Diamond is 1NT or One Spade, West will not be keen on the idea of introducing his weak heart suit at the Two level and the heart fit is likely to be lost. Only a response of One Heart leads to the right contract: West, knowing that a satisfactory trump suit has been found, has no qualms about going to the Two level with a raise to Two Hearts and East, with his minimum response is happy to pass.

You may argue that this is rather lucky. What happens, for example, if the opener has a spade suit instead of a heart suit? Perhaps:

West

♠ J 10 7 3
♥ A 5
♦ A K 7 6 4
♣ 5 2

Well, the response of One Heart works just as well as before, for over One Heart West can introduce his spade suit at the One level. Then, over the rebid of One Spade, East can give a limit raise to Two Spades (showing, as we have seen, 6–9 points); the opener knows that there cannot be the values for game and passes, and again the partnership is in the right spot.

To sum up, if you have a choice between showing a biddable suit at the One level or making a limit bid in no-trumps, the suit call works better. Furthermore, if you have a choice between two biddable suits (of the same length) that you can show at the One level, it is better to bid the lower ranking of these suits. So with:

♠ K 9 6 4
♥ Q 9 8 6
♦ 8 5
♣ Q 9 4

the response to One Diamond should be One Heart. In this way you have the best of all worlds: if partner likes hearts he can support you; if he does not like hearts but has a spade suit he can show it at the One level; and if he has neither hearts nor spades he might be in a position to bid 1NT himself.

RESPONSES AT THE TWO LEVEL

Responses in a new suit can be at the One level or the Two level, depending on the rank of partner's suit and the rank of the suit in which you want to respond. For example, over One Heart you can tell partner about a spade suit at the One level, but if you wanted to mention one of the minor suits you would have to bid Two Diamonds or Two Clubs.

A response at the One level, although of course it is forcing for the round and partner must speak again, need not contain more than the 6 points that you need to reply. A response in a new suit at the Two level, on the other hand, as it has committed the partnership to eight tricks instead of seven and is still forcing, should be based on at least 8 points.

This leads to occasional difficulties. Suppose that partner has opened One Heart and your hand is:

♠ K 8 6 4
♥ 7 4
♦ 6 4
♣ K 9 7 6 2

Your natural response (long suit first) is Two Clubs, but you are short of the required points for a Two-over-One response. The way out here is to reply One Spade, deceiving partner a little as to your distribution, but not as to your strength.

Note that with:

♠ K 8 6 4
♥ A 4
♦ 6 4
♣ K 9 7 6 2

where you have 11 points, there is no need whatsoever to resort to this expedient and you can make your natural reply of Two Clubs.

Or what about:

♠ A Q 4
♥ 5
♦ 10 8 6 4
♣ 10 7 6 3 2

after an opening bid of One Spade from partner? There are certainly not enough points to bid Two Clubs and a response of 1NT with a singleton heart would be unthinkable. Well, in spite of the principle of not supporting partner unless you hold at least four cards in his suit, the best practical bid is Two Spades. Mind you, you should have a distinct feeling of guilt at raising partner's suit with only three trumps – in an attempt to mollify your conscience you might try muddling a small club in among your spades before putting dummy down (correcting the error before partner starts to play, of course).

However, with:

♠ A Q 4
♥ 5
♦ 10 8 6 4
♣ A 7 6 3 2

you have plenty of points to make the natural call of Two Clubs over a One Spade opening bid. It is only when you have just 6 or 7 points, insufficient to call a new suit at the Two level, that you sometimes have to make a bid that seems to bend the rules a little.

To sum up:

A new suit at the One level shows 6–15 points.
A new suit at the Two level shows 8–15 points.

JUMP RESPONSES

All the responses to a suit call that have been considered so far, both limited and unlimited, have finished at 15 points. The question arises as to what action the responder should take on those happy occasions when he holds 16 or more points. The answer is that, whether he holds support for his partner's suit or not, whether he holds a balanced hand suitable for no-trumps or not, he should *jump the bidding in a new suit.*

So after the sequences One Spade – Three Diamonds, or One Diamond – Two Hearts the responder has promised at least 16 points. Don't make the mistake of thinking that if you have an *incredibly* strong hand you should make even more of a jump. No matter how many points you have, it is quite enough to bid one more than necessary. As we shall see later, a response of, say, Three Spades to One Diamond would have quite a different meaning and would in fact suggest a rather weak hand in terms of points.

These jump responses mean that game is a certainty and neither partner may pass until a game has been reached.

Suppose you held:

♠ Q 7 6
♥ A Q 9
♦ 8 5
♣ A K 8 7 6

and your partner opened One Spade. You have 15 points in high cards, 1 point for the five-card suit and another for the doubleton diamond since you have some support for your partner's spades. Knowing that your side wants to be in game, you respond Three Clubs. However, if partner simply rebids Three Spades (promising at least a five-card suit), your next bid is a simple Four Spades. Any further initiative will have to come from partner – you have already shown him the strength of your hand when you jumped to Three Clubs. Don't make the mistake of bidding your values twice!

A few more examples of jump responses are:

♠ A Q 7 3
♥ A 5
♦ 7 4
♣ A K 8 6 4

If partner opens One Spade, you are too good for a limit raise to game in spades which would suggest 13–15 points. You must start with Three Clubs, planning to support spades later.

♠ A J 10
♥ J 4 2
♦ A K J 5
♣ K 10 4

After One Heart from partner, your point count is too high to reply 3NT which again would suggest 13–15 points. You must commence with Three Diamonds and suggest no-trumps later in the auction.

♠ A K Q J 8 6 3
♥ A 5
♦ Q 7 4
♣ 6

After One Heart from partner, although you do not propose supporting his hearts or bidding no-trumps, you are altogether too strong to reply One Spade in spite of the fact that this would be forcing for one round. You must bid Two Spades to give partner a picture of the power and quality of your hand.

RESPONSES TO AN OPENING BID OF 1NT.

Most of the time when partner has opened 1NT you have no problems, particularly if you are pleased with his suggestion of no-trumps. Then bearing in mind that partner has 13–14 points, you simply raise to game if you know that you hold at least 26 points between you, and pass if you know that you have not.

However, if you are not happy with the idea of playing in no-trumps, perhaps because of a long suit and a singleton or a void elsewhere, there are at least two courses of action open to you. After hearing partner open 1NT you might find yourself with:

♠ J 8 7 6 5 2
♥ 10 7 4
♦ —
♣ 9 8 6 3

Clearly there is no chance of game, and equally clearly you are horrified by the prospect of leaving partner to play this hand in no-trumps. You would like to play in spades (remember, partner has a balanced hand and therefore at least two spades, possibly more). The natural choice would be Two Spades but you could not make this bid if there were the slightest danger of partner pressing on to 2NT or Three Diamonds or anything equally unsuitable. Nevertheless, you can bid Two Spades, for you have the absolutely firm understanding that if the bidding goes 1NT – Two of a suit, then the opening bidder passes automatically: this is known as the 'weak take-out'. Don't be worried by the fact that you haven't got enough points for a response at the Two level – that simply does not apply after a 1NT opening. All your bid says is, 'Partner, we can't make a game. I don't like no-trumps and I think that Two Spades is a better contract than 1NT. *Please pass.*'

(There is one possible exception to this: the partnership may have arranged to play the Stayman convention which will be discussed later in this chapter. If you *have* decided to play Stayman, the sequence 1NT – Two Clubs will have a special significance.)

If you are caught with a nightmare hand such as:

♠ 10 7 6 2
♥ 8 5
♦ 9 8 6 4
♣ 10 6 2

and partner opens 1NT, there is little that you can do. There is no reason to suppose that Two Diamonds or Two Spades will be any improvement on 1NT (indeed, they may be a sight worse) and all that you can do is to prepare yourself to make sympathetic noises at the end of the hand.

To bid a suit over your partner's 1NT bid guarantees at least five cards in your suit.

You won't always be dealt such bad hands. There is also the situation where you want to make an unlimited response to an opening bid of 1NT. Suppose you had started with:

♠ A K J 5 3
♥ 9
♦ K Q 7 4
♣ 9 6 5

and heard partner open 1NT. You have 13 points in high cards and an extra point for the five-card spade suit, so you certainly intend to bid game. However, it is quite possible that a Four Spade contract may be preferable to 3NT. The solution is to bid Three Spades – an unlimited bid that is forcing to at least game. You are informing partner that you have an opening bid with at least five spades. Then it is up to partner to decide what he considers to be the best contract. With only two spades in his hand he will bid 3NT on the assumption that there are only seven spades between the two hands – one short of the minimum of eight that makes a trump suit viable. With any three or more spades he will bid Four Spades.

DIFFERENTIATING BETWEEN MAJOR AND MINOR SUITS

Under another heading we have already met one distinction that we make in the bidding between major suits and minor suits, and now here is another one. With:

♠ A Q 8 6 4
♥ 7 4
♦ A 8 3
♣ A 7 4

you would respond Three Spades to an opening of 1NT, reasoning that if partner holds three or more spades there will be more safety in a contract of Four Spades than one of 3NT.

However, if you had started with:

♠ A 8 3
♥ 7 4
♦ A Q 8 6 4
♣ A 7 4

it would not be good tactics to respond Three Diamonds to 1NT. Remember that game in a minor suit requires 11 tricks as opposed to ten in one of the majors and the difference of two whole tricks between Five Diamonds and 3NT gives a strong incentive to go for game in no-trumps. Even if partner held a good fit in diamonds, the nine-trick contract would very likely prove easier.

There are circumstances in which you might want to make an unlimited response in a minor suit over 1NT, but that would usually be on the type of hand where you thought that there was a possibility your side might make a *slam* (twelve or even thirteen tricks) instead of just a game. Slam bidding will be considered in subsequent chapters.

THE STAYMAN CONVENTION

The method just discussed takes care of all good responding hands that are sufficiently unbalanced as to be uninterested in partner's suggestion of no-trumps. However, if you limit your bidding methods to what has been discussed so far, hands will come up on which you and your partner will get to the wrong contract.

Consider these hands:

	West		East
♠	A 8 3 2	♠	K Q 6 5
♥	K Q 6	♥	A 10 7 5
♦	A 3 2	♦	Q J 8 5
♣	9 8 2	♣	4

West deals and opens 1NT (with his completely balanced hand, 4-3-3-3, there is no need for him to worry about the lack of high cards in clubs) to leave East with something of a problem. He cannot bid Three of any suit for that would suggest at least a five-card suit and invite support with any three cards in the suit in West's hand. And yet if he simply raises to 3NT the partnership will clearly be in the wrong contract. No matter how the clubs divide, one opponent will hold at least five and this will be enough to defeat a contract of 3NT out of hand. Looking at the two hands you can see that Four Spades is a good proposition, but the problem remains – how can East–West get there after West has opened 1NT?

To deal with this situation a well-known American International, Sam Stayman, invented a convention. After an opening bid of 1NT the responder may initiate the Stayman convention by bidding Two Clubs. This bid is 'conventional' in the sense that it bears no relation whatsoever to the responder's holding in clubs. It simply asks the opener to bid a four-card major suit if he has one, and to say Two Diamonds if he has not. Should the opener hold length in both spades and hearts he should bid Two Hearts.

After a start of 1NT – Two Clubs, opener bids as follows:

2♦   I have no four-card major suit.
2♥   I have four hearts; it is possible that I have four spades as well.
2♠   I have four spades, but not four hearts.

Let us see how this works out on the two hands above. West opens 1NT and East, looking for a better spot than 3NT, initiates the Stayman convention by bidding Two Clubs. West has no problem in replying – he has four spades but fewer than four hearts, so he simply says Two Spades. Now East, knowing that the partnership holds at least eight spades, can safely go to Four Spades rather than take a risk on the clubs being wide open to attack in 3NT.

Consider another pair of hands:

West	*East*
♠ K Q 10 7	♠ J 9 5 3
♥ J 10 4 2	♥ 7
♦ 9 7	♦ A K J 5
♣ A K 2	♣ Q 8 5 4

West opens 1NT and East responds Two Clubs, Stayman, hoping to play in game if partner has four spades. The opener, with both hearts and spades, rebids Two Hearts. At this point East is reluctant to introduce his feeble spade suit in case partner has no support for it and just bids 2NT. After all, he has eleven points and 2NT should be safe enough now that partner is known to hold four cards in hearts. But now West has a chance to do some inferential thinking. As East has enquired for major suits and yet has no interest in hearts, he must have length in spades. So West goes on over 2NT with Three Spades. Since this is just the bid that East needs to improve his hand, he is now in a position to go on to Four Spades, an excellent contract. It is true that on the combined hands there is a fair play for 3NT, but Four Spades should be even easier.

Just in case you are getting the idea that responder can bid a Stayman Two clubs on practically any hand, here are a couple of warning examples. Suppose you hold:

♠ Q 10 7 5
♥ A J 8 3
♦ 4
♣ 10 8 7 6

You might be tempted to reply Two Clubs after partner has opened 1NT. Certainly you will strike oil if partner obliges by bidding either Two Hearts or Two Spades – you will pass (knowing that you haven't got enough for game) and you will probably be in a better contract than 1NT. But what are you going to do if partner rebids Two Diamonds, denying length in either major suit? The combined hands have perhaps 20–21 points between them – not enough to make 2NT. You are in trouble! What you should have done was to pass 1NT.

Again, with:

♠ 5
♥ Q J 8 4
♦ A J 7 3
♣ 10 9 5 2

suppose you unthinkingly respond Two Clubs to 1NT: fine if partner obliges with Two Hearts, but what are you going to do if he comes up with Two Spades? Again your partnership will have been forced out of its depth by your ill-considered action.

On both of these hands you had no real alternative to passing 1NT. You know that your side cannot make game and any attempt to improve the situation might drive you even higher in no-trumps. You can't make bricks without straw!

Before you embark on Stayman you must be sure that partner's response, whatever it is, will not embarrass you.

In case you run away with the idea that this means you cannot use Stayman on weak hands, look at the following complete deal: Dealer, East

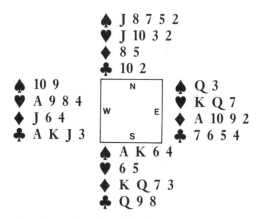

```
                    ♠ J 8 7 5 2
                    ♥ J 10 3 2
                    ♦ 8 5
                    ♣ 10 2
  ♠ 10 9          ┌──────────┐        ♠ Q 3
  ♥ A 9 8 4       │    N     │        ♥ K Q 7
  ♦ J 6 4       W │          │ E      ♦ A 10 9 2
  ♣ A K J 3       │    S     │        ♣ 7 6 5 4
                  └──────────┘
                    ♠ A K 6 4
                    ♥ 6 5
                    ♦ K Q 7 3
                    ♣ Q 9 8
```

After a pass by East, South with his balanced 14 points opened 1NT. Although West himself had an opening bid, the 1NT opening on his right made it difficult for him to join in and there was no good alternative to a pass. (This highlights one of the big advantages in opening 1NT rather than One of a suit – any action that the opponents take will have to be at the Two level.) Now consider North's problem. He had a terrible hand with only 2 points facing his partner's 13–14 points. Clearly his side was out-gunned. He could have said Two Spades, expecting this to be an improvement on 1NT, but North saw no reason why he should not use Stayman. After all, if partner responded Two Spades or Two Hearts, North would be delighted to pass, and if the worst happened and South was forced to reply Two Diamonds, denying length in either major suit, then North could still go to Two Spades. In any event, North could not be worse off than if he had responded Two Spades immediately. (Note the essential difference between this and the last two hands we looked at – in this case North was in a position to take care of any response his partner made.)

As it was, the unexpected happened. After a pass by East, South was able to oblige with a bid of Two Spades. West passed and North was delighted to do likewise. So Two Spades became the final contract and West led the Ace of clubs. The play was not difficult. With the trumps falling in two rounds declarer was able to make five spade tricks, together with two heart ruffs in his own hand after losing the first two tricks in the suit. In addition the King and Queen of diamonds were between them worth another trick. In all South lost two hearts, two clubs and a diamond to make his contract – a fine result with only 16 points to the opponents' 24 points. As the cards lay East–West could have made at least nine tricks with clubs as trumps, if they had been able to get safely into the bidding!

Try bidding the following hands after your partner has opened 1NT:

	a		*b*		*c*
♠	8 5	♠	8 5	♠	8 5
♥	A Q J 6 4	♥	A Q J 6	♥	A Q J 6
♦	K 10 6 4	♦	K 10 6 4 2	♦	Q 10 6 4
♣	K 3	♣	K 3	♣	8 7 3

a. Three Hearts is best. You are not interested in whether partner has got *four* hearts or not, so you don't want to use Stayman. All that concerns you is whether he has got *three* or more hearts.

b. Two Clubs is best. Again, you have enough for game. This time, if partner has four hearts, game in this suit will be best. If he hasn't, then you will settle for 3NT. There should be no temptation to show the diamonds.

c. No Bid. And quickly! You have not got enough for game, and there is little point in trying to improve the contract. To use Stayman might be disastrous if partner were to reply Two Spades.

7.   Rebids and reverses

After an opening suit call at the One level and an unlimited response in a new suit, neither player has made a bid that in any way limits his hand. For example, after the start of One Heart – One Spade the opener is known to hold something between 13 and 20 points and the responder something between 6 and 15 points. Between them, this spans quite a range. It could be that the partnership have only 19 points and are just looking for a suit that both partners like before they drop the bidding as quickly as possible; it could be that they hold as many as 35 points, in which case they will set their sights higher than game and consider bidding a small or even a grand slam. Furthermore, neither player has, as yet, any clear picture of what *type* of hand his partner holds. Either one may be one-suited, two-suited or even balanced.

With his rebid the opener must strive to do two things – tell his partner what *type* of hand he holds, and attempt to get over some picture of whether he has a weak, medium or strong opening bid. Much of the time, we will find, he can achieve both of these objects by making a limit bid.

There are four main headings under which the opener's rebid may be classified. He can choose from these possibilities:

1. Supporting partner's suit.
2. Rebidding in no-trumps.
3. Rebidding his own suit.
4. Bidding a new suit.

Only one thing is certain: that the opener must make a rebid. As we have seen, no matter how weak his opening bid, it is possible that partner may hold enough for them to make game. (It is as well to remind ourselves again that this does *not* apply if the responder has made a limit bid: then the opener may well be in a position to judge that his side are short of game-going values.)

Sometimes the opener will have to exercise judgement as to which of the four courses of action is best fitted to his particular hand, but most of the time his decision will be quite clear cut. Let's consider the possibilities one at a time.

SUPPORTING PARTNER'S SUIT

As usual, you should be extremely reluctant to raise your partner's suit with fewer than four cards. Suppose the bidding has started West – One Heart, East – One Spade and as West you hold:

♠ Q 9 7 3
♥ A Q 8 6 4
♦ A 7
♣ 4 3

You have only a minimum opening in terms of high cards so, in spite of your evident liking for partner's suit, you don't want to do anything that will excite him too much. To raise to Two Spades is quite sufficient, suggesting that your opening bid was in the range of 13–15 points.

Next, imagine that your hand has been strengthened by the addition of another Ace – becoming a whole trick better. Say:

♠ Q 9 7 3
♥ A Q 8 6 4
♦ A 7
♣ A 3

Naturally enough you still open One Heart but after East's response of One Spade you will want to take more ambitious action than the single raise that you found last time. Three Spades is the answer, showing a hand with 16–18 points in support of spades.

Again, improve the West hand still more to become:

♠ K J 9 7
♥ A Q 8 6 4
♦ A 7
♣ A 3

You still open One Heart, for there will be no future in the hand unless partner is strong enough (6 points) to find a response.

However, things brighten enormously once you have heard a response of One Spade from East. In support of spades your hand is worth 21 points and no matter how weak East was for his original response you want to be in game. You bid Four Spades, showing a minimum of 19 points in support of spades.

Raising partner's suit after you have opened is very similar to supporting opener's suit – the more you have, the more you bid. Furthermore, although bidding such as West – One Heart, East – One Spade, West – Three Spades sounds tremendously encouraging, that is all it is – encouraging. It is *not* forcing partner to speak again; if he has scraped up his original One Spade reply on a bare 6 or 7 points then it should be easy for him to judge that with your announced 16–18 points the partnership will be short of game values and so say No Bid.

REBIDDING IN NO-TRUMPS

Just like opening bids in no-trumps, just like responses in no-trumps, any rebid in no-trumps can only be made on a *balanced* hand. Take care to avoid rebidding no-trumps with a singleton in partner's suit just because you have the other three suits well represented. This is an easy trap to fall into, but one that you should try to avoid at all costs. It is tempting, but this is another temptation that must be resisted. If you are still not convinced, consider a suit like this:

West	*East*
2	A Q 10 6 5

Imagine yourself playing in a no-trump contract with this as one of your suits. How many tricks will it be worth to your side? One? Two, perhaps if you are a good guesser. But now change the West holding to J 2:

West	*East*
J 2	A Q 10 6 5

Now you are faced with a suit that will not just bring in one or two tricks – instead it should yield four tricks, even against a 4-2 break of the opponents' cards in the suit. On your lucky days, you may even make all five tricks (King in the North hand, the missing si cards divided 3-3). What a difference if you have got something of a *fit* in partner's suit, instead of a singleton. You can then *use* partner's suit to develop tricks.

Suppose that after the same start of West – One Heart, East – One Spade, West's hand is as follows:

♠ J 2
♥ A Q 10 7
♦ K Q 9 5
♣ K 10 9

He was too strong to open 1NT (which would show 13-14 points). He had no choice but to open One Heart. Now, however, after the response of One Spade, the *rebid* of 1NT is more descriptive than Two Diamonds and shows 15-16 points.

But suppose West had started with a stronger hand, say:

♠ K 2
♥ A Q 10 7
♦ K Q 9 5
♣ K 10 9

As before, he steps up his rebid by one level and says 2NT over a One Spade response, showing 17-18 points. It is worth noting that if East-West had arranged to play the *Strong* No-trump (which will be referred to later), West could have opened the bidding with 1NT. Of course, when making a rebid in no-trumps, West cannot count any distributional points for shortages.

Finally, if West's hand had been:

♠ K 2
♥ A Q 10 7
♦ K Q 9 5
♣ K Q 10

he would have been too strong even for a Strong No-trump and yet not good enough to start with 2NT. He still just opens One Heart; but when partner responds One Spade, guaranteeing at least 6 points, West is prepared to have a shot at game. The rebid of 3NT shows 19 points.

REBIDDING HIS OWN SUIT

A simple rebid of the opener's suit at the Two level, e.g. One Heart, One Spade, Two Hearts is quite the most discouraging rebid that he can find. It is the one that is designed to pour cold water on any ambitious schemes responder may have. True, it promises extra length in the rebid suit (at least five cards) but it denies the ability to make a more constructive rebid, such as supporting partner, bidding no-trumps, or showing a new suit. However, it is very necessary to have a safety-valve of this nature. Everyone likes to open hands such as:

♠ K 6
♥ A J 10 9 7 5
♦ K 8 3
♣ 7 4

Only 11 high card points here but the 2 extra points for the six-card suit just turn the scale – you can't afford to do so if every time your partner holds a couple of Aces and a King he goes crashing on to game. However, the simple rebid of your own suit strictly limits your holding to 13–15 points and suggests that your hand is one suited.

It is certainly true that higher rebids in the opener's suit still suggest one-suited hands and that, following the pattern we have seen developing, the sequence One Heart – One Spade, Three Hearts would suggest something like 16–18 points and the rebid to Four Hearts even more; but there is something rather special about these rebids. On previous occasions when you have jumped the bidding, albeit with a limit bid, you have had the assurance that you were in a sensible contract, either supporting partner with a known trump fit, or rebidding in no-trumps with a balanced hand. One thing is sure: if you introduce a jump rebid in your own suit you must have a good and *independent* suit, for partner has promised nothing in the way of support with his reply in a new suit. An independent suit is one which a player is fully prepared to play with as trumps even if partner turns up with a doubleton or a small singleton.

So with:

♠ K 6
♥ A K Q 9 7 5
♦ K 8 3
♣ 7 4

you would be prepared to rebid Three Hearts over a response of
One Spade. You have 17 points, allowing for the long suit, and
would be quite prepared to play with hearts as trumps even if
partner has very little in the suit.

BIDDING A NEW SUIT

Just as when we considered responding in a new suit rather than
making a limit bid in reply to an opening bid, so the scene changes
slightly at this point. All the previous rebids have been limit bids,
describing both the type of hand that the opener holds as well as
defining his strength to within narrow limits. But when it comes to
bidding a new suit, there is the same sort of difficulty that we en-
countered before. Just because you happen to hold 19 points, you
cannot consider starting the auction with One Heart, One Spade,
Four Diamonds just to show your strength as well as your other
suit. In principle, at any rate, when you are bidding a new suit as
opener you do not rush things.
    So with:

♠ K 6
♥ A J 10 7 6
♦ K J 6 5
♣ 6 3

you would rebid Two Diamonds if your One Heart opening bid
met with a One Spade response. But equally with:

♠ K 6
♥ A J 10 7 6
♦ K J 6 5
♣ A 6

you would still rebid Two Diamonds. A simple rebid in a new suit
can be made on a hand with 13–18 points; it is only when the hand
is as strong as 19–20 points that special action has to be taken. With
a hand of this strength you *know* that your side should end in game

as soon as you hear a response from partner. If you plan to support partner's suit or rebid in no-trumps, then you have no worries, you can *bid* game. But if you intend to bid a new suit, then you no longer know what game it is that you want to bid. The solution is very straight-forward. If you have started with 19 points and decide to make your rebid in a new suit, then you *jump* the bidding, making your bid at one level higher than you would normally. For example, One Heart, One Spade, *Three* Clubs or One Diamond, One Heart, *Two* Spades. Just like the jump in a new suit when you are responding, this jump in a new suit informs your partner that between you there are sufficient values for game. Neither member of the partnership may now pass until game has been reached.

If you had started with:

♠ A J 6
♥ A K 7 6 3
♦ A K 9 4
♣ 5

you would open One Heart. If partner responds One Spade, you know that you have the values for game between the two hands. But you do not know, as yet, in *what* game that you want to play. At this stage it might be game in hearts, spades, diamonds or even no-trumps! However, you rebid Three Diamonds, telling partner about your other suit and at the same time letting him know the full strength of your hand. Whatever partner bids next (and remember, he is forced to go on) will help you. He might rebid his spades, showing at least five cards in the suit – then you can go on to Four Spades, secure in the knowledge that a trump suit with at least eight cards between the two hands has been found. He might be in a position to support your diamonds; he might have the clubs well held and be able to call no-trumps. Finally, he may bid Three Hearts. Now, you know that he does not hold four hearts in his hand – he had the opportunity of supporting hearts on the first round and yet did not do so. But if he subsequently puts you back to your suit you at least know that he has a tolerance for the suit, probably three-card support. Then Four Hearts is likely to be the best final contract.

A player will often have a choice between rebidding his own suit and bidding a new suit. Suppose that he has a minimum hand;

then although the rebid of his own suit at the lowest possible level shows 13–15 points whereas a bid of a new suit is still fairly un-limited (13–18 points) it is usually best to show the new suit *if he can do so conveniently.*

Suppose you had started with:

♠ A 6
♥ A K 6 5 3
♦ Q 10 7 5
♣ 6 2

After the start of One Heart, One Spade, a rebid of Two Diamonds stands to be far more helpful as far as partner is concerned than the uninformative rebid of Two Hearts. Partner may hold a fairly balanced hand with perhaps only **J** x in diamonds – then your call will enable him to bid no-trumps.

Don't carry this principle too far. With:

♠ A 6
♥ A K Q J 10
♦ 5 4 3 2
♣ 6 2

after the same start of One Heart, One Spade, there is no sensible alternative to Two Hearts. Your other suit should be biddable before it is worth showing.

You will have noticed that it has been suggested that a second suit should be shown if this is *convenient.* This leads to a topic about which there are more mistaken ideas than any other in bridge.

REVERSES

Not all rebids in new suits are weak – there is a class of rebids that, although no strength-showing jump is involved, suggests hands that are appreciably better than minimum, both in points and distribution.

Here is an example:

♠ A K J 4
♥ A Q 10 7 3
♦ K 5 2
♣ 8

With 17 points in high cards and 1 distributional point, making a total of 18 points, the hand is opened naturally with a bid of One Heart. Now suppose partner responds Two Clubs. This has not improved the opener's hand in any way (a shortage in partner's suit is usually more of a liability rather than an asset), but the opener still has a very strong hand. He follows with a bid of Two Spades. Now consider the implications of this bid:

a. The opener must be showing a hand with *more* hearts than spades. If he had held four spades and four hearts he would have opened with the higher ranking of two touching suits, i.e. spades. If he had held five spades and five hearts he would have opened with the higher ranking suit, spades. But in this case he has bid his suits in 'reverse' order – lower ranking first, followed by the higher ranking.

b. The opener cannot have a weak hand, for if responder simply wants to put him back to his first suit he must do so at the Three level. Remembering that responder need not have all that much in terms of high cards, the opener should be quite strong before he is prepared to play the hand at the Three level. A sensible lower limit to fix on a reverse bid of this nature is 16 points.

It is important to remember that you do not reverse to show strength alone; and you do not reverse to show distribution alone.
Before you make a reverse bid, your hand must have both of these requirements.

It is quite possible that the opener has five cards in his second (and higher ranking) suit. But in that case, as he has promised **more** cards in his first suit, he must have a 6–5 distribution in his two suits. Suppose you had started with:

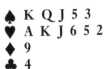

♠ K Q J 5 3
♥ A K J 6 5 2
♦ 9
♣ 4

The opening bid is One Heart (longest suit first, naturally enough), and over a response of Two Clubs the hand is worth a reverse to Two Spades as before. But now when partner makes another bid, say 2NT, you can complete the picture of your distribution by bidding spades again. Partner will then know that you have five spades (five cards is the minimum length you must hold for a suit to be rebiddable) and hence at least six hearts (for by reversing you have told him that your first, lower ranking suit is *longer* than your second suit). With three bids you have conveyed a very precise picture of your hand, both as regards distribution and strength.

If you had been dealt:

♠ A K 7 6
♥ A Q 10 7
♦ A 7 5
♣ 5 3

what would you open? Yes, quite right, One Spade. Although you have all the necessary strength for a reverse, you have not got more cards in the hearts than the spades and you have no alternative but to bid the hand naturally, starting with the higher ranking of two touching four-card suits.

Equally, if you had been dealt:

♠ A J 5 2
♥ Q J 9 7 3
♦ K Q 6
♣ 8

you would open One Heart (longest suit first). But if partner's response is Two Clubs or Two Diamonds (in spite of the fact that the latter response improves your hand) you are not strong enough to reverse with Two Spades. With only 13 high card points and 1 for distribution you are 2 points short of the minimum of 16 that you need. There is no choice now but to rebid Two Hearts.

Sometimes your ability to show your second suit will depend upon the response that partner chooses. For example:

♠ A Q 5 4
♥ 9 3
♦ A J 10 7 5 4
♣ 2

With 11 points in high cards and an extra 2 for your six-card suit you open One Diamond. If partner bids One Heart, you can quite properly rebid One Spade. This is *not* a reverse bid, as partner does not have to bid at the Three level to tell you which suit he prefers.

In fact, there is no such thing as a reverse at the One level.

However, if partner had chosen to respond Two Clubs instead of One Heart, your spade suit would have to go unmentioned for the time being. A bid of Two Spades would be a reverse, as partner would have to go to Three Diamonds before he could tell you that he preferred your diamonds. Over Two Clubs, therefore, you have no choice but to rebid Two Diamonds.

EFFECTS OF THE OPPONENTS' BIDDING

There is one rather deceptive situation that is worth mentioning at this point. So far, in the discussion on bidding, the opponents have not joined in at all. They have only been there to deal the cards, say No Bid when it is their turn to speak, and say 'Well done!' or 'Bad luck!' at the end of each hand. Real life at the bridge table is not like that – the opponents often join in the bidding, sometimes quite inconveniently.

Take this hand:

♠ 8 7.
♥ A Q 6 5
♦ 7 4
♣ A K 9 8 7

You open One Club and, assuming the opposition remain silent, plan to rebid One Heart over a response of One Diamond (not a reverse, as we have seen) and Two Clubs over a response of One Spade (to bid Two Hearts now would, of course, be a reverse). Apparently no problems, but suppose someone does join in? If you were West, the bidding might go:

West	North	East	South
1♣	1♠	2♦	pass

You can't pass, for partner has responded in a new suit. The problem is to decide whether a bid of Two Hearts at this point would constitute a reverse. Superficially, yes, for it forces partner to tell you which of your suits he prefers at the Three level. But when you think of it, *your* bidding was not responsible for this situation. It was *partner* who bid Two Diamonds as a result of the intervention and so raised the level. If you bid Two Hearts now, all you are saying is that you were planning to rebid One Heart over One Diamond had there been no interference. Indeed, Two Hearts is a *cheaper* call than rebidding the clubs by saying Three Clubs. Only one thing is certain – partner, who was responsible for this situation, must have sensibly more points than he would have needed to respond at the One level. He has bid at the Two level and in a suit higher ranking than the opener's and must have the values to make this safe.

RESPONDER'S ACTION AFTER HEARING A REVERSE BY OPENER

As we have seen a player who has made a reverse bid has painted a very clear picture of his hand, both as regards strength and distribution. It should be possible for the responder to take advantage of this. Perhaps this is best illustrated with the aid of example hands. Suppose the opening bid has been made on the hand that we started with:

♠ A K J 4
♥ A Q 10 7 3
♦ K 5 2
♣ 8

and that in each case the bidding has gone West – One Heart, East – Two Clubs, West – Two Spades. If East held:

♠ 7 6
♥ 5 4 2
♦ 8 7 6
♣ A K 10 8 7

he would have nothing in reserve. He has, after all, already promised at least 8 points by responding at the Two level. In spite of the fact that West has shown at least 16 points, East cannot do more than tell his partner that he prefers his hearts to his spades by bidding Three Hearts. But if East had a stronger hand:

♠ 7 6
♥ K 4 2
♦ 8 7 6
♣ A K 10 8 7

then a bid of Three Hearts would be altogether too cautious. East knows that the partnership hold at least 16+11 points between them, and that they hold at least eight hearts in the two hands. There is no reason for East to hold back and the correct bid is Four Hearts.

Again, if East had started with:

♠ 7 6
♥ 4 2
♦ Q 10 7 6
♣ A J 10 8 7

he is in a position where he does not think highly of either of his partner's suits. With nothing in hand (he has already shown 8 points) he is not prepared to make another forward-going bid, and yet it would be foolish to say No Bid and leave partner in Two Spades. West might well hold only a four-card spade suit and in that case spades would be a most unsatisfactory trump suit. Instead, East can suggest that he has some values in diamonds (the only unbid suit) by bidding 2NT at this point. Note that this would not show the 10-12 points that you would expect if partner had shown nothing more than the 13 he needed to open, but takes advantage of the fact that the opener has by this time shown a minimum of 16 points.

If East had started with a similar but stronger hand:

♠ 7 6
♥ 4 2
♦ Q J 10 8
♣ A K 10 8 7

then to bid 2NT (after partner had promised at least 16) would again be too unambitious. With the unbid suit of diamonds well held and with the knowledge that the two hands have full game-going values, there is no excuse for not bidding 3NT.

There is a lot to be said for the old bridge saying, 'Bid what you think you can make!'

Finally, if East's hand was:

♠ 7 6
♥ 4 2
♦ 8 7 6
♣ A Q J 10 7 6

he would again be in the position of having no good fit in either of partner's suits. But now he has no guard in diamonds, so a bid in no-trumps would no longer be acceptable. However, the club suit is very long and strong (so strong that you would not be too distressed if partner turned out to hold perhaps a low singleton in the suit) and is worth bidding again. By saying Three Clubs East affirms a suit of this quality, denies values in diamonds, and expresses dislike for both of partner's suits. As we saw in considering opener's rebid, a rebid of the same suit by a player is always rather a depressing move.

8.   Defensive bidding

Half the time in bridge either you or your partner will end up by playing the hand; the remaining half of the time you will be defending. To be successful at bridge you want to be as sure as possible that when your side plays the hand you are in the right contract – whether it is a part-score, a game, or a slam. In other words, when you and your partner have stronger hands than the opponents, you want to make the best of them. However, and just as important, if the hand 'belongs' to the opposition you must attempt to prevent them playing in their best contract. Perhaps you can push them to too high a contract; perhaps you can make it difficult for them to find the right suit in which to play; and even if you can't achieve either of these ends, it might be possible to suggest to your partner what you would like him to lead to get the defence off to the best possible start.

All the bidding theory that we have discussed up to now has been based on the assumption that the opponents stay silent. It would be simply splendid if they guaranteed to do just that, but in real life their activities during the auction can be distinctly irritating. It is important for us to consider how we can achieve the above objects if an *opponent* opens the bidding. There are no fewer than five different types of defensive action that you can take:

1. Overcalling in a suit.
2. Overcalling in no-trumps.
3. Making a jump overcall.
4. Making a take-out double.
5. Making a pre-emptive bid.

(To let you in on a secret in advance, as if these were not enough alternatives, there is indeed a sixth course of action that you could take – a bid in the opponent's suit. But we will touch on this possibility later when we consider the ways in which a player can show his partner an enormously strong hand.)

OVERCALLING IN A SUIT

The requirements for an opening bid are quite specific (at least 13 points, counting both honour points and distribution points), and in a way the requirements for an overcall in a suit are even more precise. The most important thing is safety. When you join in the bidding (after an opening bid of One of a suit on your right), the opponent on your left may hold some strength and length in the suit that you have bid. *And he knows that his partner has got the values for an opening bid.* In these circumstances it will be easy for him to double you and extract a resounding penalty, perhaps much larger in value than if he and his partner had bid and made a game. The same is not true when *you* open the bidding – then the opposition have not had a chance to get together and it is most unlikely that either opponent on his own will be in a position to judge that his side will do best by extracting a penalty. Compare the following two hands:

	a		*b*
♠	K Q J 10 7 6	♠	7 6 5
♥	6 4	♥	A 8 4
♦	K 7 6	♦	A 6 3
♣	8 3	♣	A J 3 2

Suppose in each case the bidding has been opened One Diamond by the player on your right. With hand *a* you have not got enough points for an opening bid – if you had dealt the cards you would have passed. But over an opening bid of One Diamond the hand is a perfectly sound overcall of One Spade. It is a *safe* bid. With diamonds called on your right you expect ♦K to score, and with spades as trumps you have five virtually certain tricks. If the worst happens and you are doubled and find dummy with no values to speak of, you should be delighted. You will come to six tricks and lose a penalty of perhaps 100 points. However, the opponents will have collected only 100 points on a deal where they had started with about 30 honour points between them – easily enough for a game!

On the other hand, with hand *b* you have started with enough points for an opening bid in your own right. After a pass by your right-hand opponent you would undoubtedly have started with 1NT or, if playing the strong no-trump, One Club. But after One Diamond on your right, what can you consider bidding? Two Clubs? Just imagine what would happen to you if you were doubled and found nothing of any great use to you in the dummy. In your hand, with clubs as trumps, you have the expectation of making only three tricks with your three Aces. It is a bit much to expect partner, who hasn't had a chance to say a word yet, to supply the missing five tricks!

Hand *a* is not an opening bid, but it is a sound overcall. Hand *b*, although a perfectly sensible opening bid, doesn't begin to be a sound overcall. This then is the crunch: when you overcall an opponent's bid in a suit, then regardless of your point count, you should have a *good suit* with a fair amount of playing strength. And the minimum length in a suit for an overcall is *five cards*.

Take another example hand:

♠ A K Q 5 3
♥ Q 7
♦ 8 5 2
♣ 9 3 2

If you had the opportunity to start the auction, you would pass as you have not got an opening bid: you have 11 honour points and 1 distributional point for the five-card suit. But the hand qualifies for a simple overcall at the One level, so if the opponent on your right opens the bidding with One Club, One Diamond or One Heart you can call One Spade. If partner has some values of his own he may be able to support you or bid a suit of his own. And even if he hasn't got a great deal and the opponents later buy the contract, partner will know that you have strength in spades and may be able to lead one, which he might not have done if you had not bid. And as far as you are concerned, you would far rather that partner led spades against any contract the opposition won than any other suit!

Overcalls can be at the Two level as well as at the One level. Suppose you had begun with:

♠ 6 5 4
♥ K Q 10 9 5
♦ A 7 4
♣ 8 3

Over One Club or One Diamond you would be happy to join in with a bid of One Heart - nothing terrible can happen to you if you are only committed to take seven tricks. But if the opening bid on your right had been One Spade, you would have second thoughts as to the wisdom of making a bid. You would be committing your side to eight tricks by bidding at the Two level, and a pass would be more prudent.

It is far better to make an overcall with 7 or 8 honour points and a good suit than one with perhaps 13 points and a suit with many possible losers.

Just consider this hand:

♠ 6 3
♥ K 7
♦ Q J 10 9 6 4
♣ A 7 5

Only 10 honour points, but with diamonds as trumps a good hand from the point of playing tricks. You have four tricks in diamonds - look at the solidity of the suit Q, J, 10, 9. Tens and nines don't count as points when we are assessing the hand, but they bolster the ability to take tricks if that suit is trumps.

Consider an extreme case:

a	*b*
A K 4 3 2	Q J 10 9 8

With this suit as trumps the holding *a*, which contains 7 honour points, can only *guarantee* two tricks. On the other hand *b*, irrespective of how the other cards in the suit are shared out, ensures three certain tricks if it is the trump suit. And yet *b* contains only 3 honour points!

As has been suggested, a player who overcalls is always taking something of a risk, but provided that he has a certain amount of playing strength the possible rewards should be worth the risk. We have already seen that an overcall can direct partner's attention to the lead that you want. There is also the possibility of being able to push the opposition just too high. For example the opponents might, if uninterrupted, bid One Heart – Two Hearts, all pass, and make just eight tricks for their contract. But if you had been able to overcall the One Heart opening with One Spade and your partner had been able to contest with Two Spades over Two Hearts, you would have put pressure on the other side. Either they let you play in Two Spades, perhaps making, or they are forced to go on to Three Hearts which may be one too high for their combined resources.

Even if your partner has a poor hand in terms of high cards it may be one that will produce a lot of tricks if he has a good fit in your suit. Then it might be possible to outbid the opponents even if you don't think that you will make your final contract. Suppose that the opposition can make ten tricks with hearts as trumps, that they are vulnerable and that making game in hearts will give them game and rubber. Your side may not be able to make ten tricks in spades, but if you can make nine or even eight it will be worth while pushing on, for to go one down doubled is far cheaper than conceding the rubber. And on your lucky days the opposition, determined not to be cheated out of their heritage, will press on to Five Hearts. Then, if they still make only ten tricks, you will find yourself recording a plus score of a hand on which it seemed that your side was outgunned. We call bidding something that you don't really expect to make a *sacrifice bid*; but mind you, only go in for sacrifices with a certain amount of discretion. No partner is going to be pleased with a long string of 800s and 1100s written down in the column of the score sheet marked 'They' even if we are able to claim proudly 'We saved the rubber!'

There is another possible advantage to joining in that we haven't considered yet. If your right-hand opponent opens One Heart an overcall of One Spade by you will not really inconvenience your other opponent. Whatever he was planning to bid, he can still bid. And should it be that he was contemplating a response in spades, he can always double you. However, suppose the opening bid was One Club. Your left-hand opponent might be planning to respond in hearts or diamonds, but if you are able to intervene with a bid of One Spade you will be making life difficult for him. Before he can show either of his red suits he will have to respond at the Two level, and in a suit higher ranking than his partner's. Some of the time he simply won't have the values to bid at this increased level, and the position can arise where perhaps hearts is the opposition's best contract, but neither of them has a chance to mention the suit.

Before all the possible advantages of overcalling go to your head remember, you must have a *good suit* to provide the necessary measure of safety.

OVERCALLING IN NO-TRUMPS

Earlier on, we looked at this hand:

♠ 7 6 5
♥ A 8 4
♦ A 6 3
♣ A J 3 2

and considered action that could be taken over an opening bid of One Diamond by the right-hand opponent. We rejected the possibility of overcalling in clubs for the simple reason that we did not have any real guarantee of making more than three tricks if we played the hand with clubs as trumps. What, then, about over-calling with 1NT? Certainly the hand would have been worth an *opening bid* of 1NT. Again, the answer is that such action would be too dangerous. If left-hand opponent had started with 8, 9 points or more it would be easy for him to double 1NT, for he would know (having heard his partner open the bidding) that his side held more than half the points in the pack. And it is very difficult to make tricks in a no-trump contract without points. The situation is very different from when the overcaller has a long and good trump suit to protect him from a large penalty. Before a player can risk making an overcall in no-trumps he must have a firm point-count, and the usually accepted standard is 16-18 points (the same values as a player needs for a strong 1NT opening). Furthermore, the no-trump overcaller must have at least one guard in the opponent's suit and preferably two.

Suppose you had been dealt:

♠ K J 5
♥ A 3
♦ K Q J 7
♣ Q J 8 6

and that the bidding had been opened on your right with One Spade. The hand is quite suitable for a 1NT overcall: first, it is balanced with no long suits and no short suits, in particular no singletons or voids; second, it contains 17 points, fitting into the 16–18 range that partner will expect; and third, it contains at least one guard (possibly two) in spades – the suit bid by the opponent on the right. Of course there is no guarantee that you will make 1NT – it is still possible that you will be doubled, find partner with nothing, and be scrambling for tricks. However, the safety factor is present; even if partner has a terrible hand you won't go too many off, and it is always possible that he may have a long suit and be able to stage a rescue act.

Nevertheless, just because you have what seems to be a suitable hand with the right number of points, this does not mean that you have to join in without any further ado. Suppose you hold exactly the same hand as in the last example, but that this time the bidding is opened on your left with One Diamond. Your partner passes, and right-hand opponent responds with One Heart. You still have 17 points, but the opening bidder has shown 13 points and could, of course, hold more. Right-hand opponent has shown 6 points with his response and he, too, might well have more. One thing is certain before you start – your partner will have very little indeed. To bid here might easily land you in a death trap, sandwiched between two opponents. Although it may go against the grain with a lot of players ('What? Pass with 17 points?'), it is certainly the wisest thing to do at this point.

MAKING A JUMP OVERCALL

The question arises as to what action you should take after an opening bid on your right if you hold such a hand as:

♠ A K Q 10 9 3
♥ K 7
♦ A 6 4
♣ 3 2

One thing is certain: your hand is far too good for a simple over-call of One Spade – that would be a bid that you might make with both of your Aces replaced by low cards! The solution is to bid Two

Spades – *a jump overcall* – taking the bidding exactly one level higher than necessary. This is a bid based on a strong suit in a strong hand and is made when you hope to take the offensive and perhaps be able to make a game. This jump overcall guarantees at least a good six-card suit and also suggests a hand with some defensive strength outside, equipped to punish the opponents if they get too high. It is not forcing; in other words partner is quite free to pass if he has nothing, but it is strongly invitational. Consider the example above: as the missing Ace of hearts is likely to be with the opening bidder, other things being equal, the King of hearts can be upgraded. Even if partner has nothing at all, you would expect to make seven or eight tricks on your own. What is more, your spade suit is *independent*; should the worst happen and partner turn up with a small singleton in the suit, it is still quite playable as a trump suit. Finally, with three or four likely tricks in *defence* you are altogether too strong to try one of the pre-emptive bids that we will be discussing.

After a jump overcall of Two Spades, partner will have a very clear picture of your hand (seven or eight winners, an independent suit), and it will not be too difficult for him to make an intelligent decision.

Suppose that, facing a jump overcall of Two Spades, you hold:

♠ 8 6
♥ A 6 5
♦ K 8 5
♣ Q 8 6 5 4

You have 9 honour points, which should be enough for game opposite a jump overcall. And what is more, you are quite happy with the idea of spades as trumps. Partner has promised a good six-card suit, so you know that you have eight trumps between you. You have the right material to raise directly to Four Spades (not Three Spades, which partner might pass. *You* know there is enough for game; *partner* doesn't). Look at this hand in conjunction with the last example: there should be two hearts, two diamonds and six spade tricks unless you run into a 4–1 spade break – well against the odds.

You can also employ a jump overcall in a minor suit, inviting partner to try for game in no-trumps or continue in your suit.

Suppose your right-hand opponent opens One Spade and you hold:

♠ 3
♥ A 4
♦ A K Q J 8 5
♣ J 7 5 2

Again you have a very good suit, this time presumably with no losers. The bid of Three Diamonds, a single jump overcall, describes this sort of hand well. However, there is the vital difference between major and minor suits that we have met several times already – even if a partnership have a good fit in a *minor* suit, they must always remember that they will need to come to eleven tricks before they can make game with their suit as trumps. If it is at all possible to play the hands in no-trumps, only nine tricks will be needed for game. With the above hand you can supply what looks like seven certain tricks, so if partner has a guard in the opponent's suit, spades, and perhaps a high card somewhere else in the hand, 3NT could be an easy make.

If, for example, he holds:

♠ A 7 5
♥ K 3 2
♦ 6 4 3
♣ 9 8 6 4

he would bid 3NT in reply to Three Diamonds. This contract would be undefeatable (or, to use a bridge expression, 'cold') – there are nine top winners with the Ace of spades, the Ace and King of hearts and six diamond tricks. At worst the opposition could take four club tricks. And yet these two hands can only come to ten tricks if they play with diamonds as trumps. In spite of the solid trump suit, there is no way of avoiding at least three losers in clubs, even if the opponents don't find a club lead immediately.

When you make a jump overcall there are certain inferences that partner can draw. He knows that you haven't the balanced type of hand on which you might have overcalled 1NT; he knows that you haven't the all-round type of hand, short in the opponent's suit, on which you would have made a takeout double (discussed in the next section); but he also knows that you have a hand which is primarily one-suited with some honours outside the suit. If he has a good suit of his own in a hand with few high cards he might well bid the suit. You won't necessarily have a fit for his suit but if you do have a tolerance for it, say Ace and another or indeed any doubleton honour, you can raise partner's new suit.

Take the hand of the last example:

♠ 3
♥ A 4
♦ A K Q J 8 5
♣ J 7 5 2

You will remember that right-hand opponent opened the bidding with One Spade and that you made a jump overcall of Three Diamonds. Suppose the next player passes and partner bids Three Hearts. He knows that you have a good hand, but you haven't promised any support for hearts at all. He may not be too strong in terms of high cards, but one thing is certain: he has a good heart suit. And so you are well placed to raise Three Hearts to Four Hearts. He might have a hand like this:

♠ 8 5 4
♥ K Q J 10 7 5
♦ 6 3
♣ 8 4

As you can see, putting the two hands together, there are plenty of winners in a heart contract, and the opponents can take only three tricks quickly.

To take another example, suppose you had started with:

♠ K 5
♥ 5
♦ K 9 8 2
♣ A K Q 10 6 5

Over One Heart on your right you would make a jump overcall of Three Clubs. Then partner, with:

♠ A Q J 10 8 4
♥ 9 8 7
♦ Q 5 3
♣ 2

would be able to show his suit with a call of Three Spades, which you would be happy to raise to Four Spades. Of course, sometimes you will have no fit at all in the suit partner suggests: then you will have little option but to return to your own suit as economically as possible.

You will frequently be faced with a situation where your right-hand opponent opens the bidding and you find yourself with an opening bid or better but no good suit of your own. Perhaps the lack of a guard or a stopper in the opponent's suit, or the wrong number of points, makes an overcall of 1NT unthinkable – something like this:

♠ K J 10 5
♥ 6
♦ K 8 7 4
♣ A K 5 3

when you hear an opening bid of One Heart on your right. Before you learned that a simple suit overall promised a good five-card suit, you might have considered bidding One Spade, or Two Clubs or even Two Diamonds. However, you will now appreciate that two things are wrong with any of these courses of action. Your suit is not long enough and your partner is unlikely to place you with as many points as this if all you can muster is a simple overcall. Furthermore, to choose any one suit would be putting all your eggs in one basket. Suppose you chose to call One Spade and found partner with a hand containing a singleton spade and five or six clubs but very few points. Without values he would be unable to do anything about it and you would play ingloriously in the wrong contract.

What you would like to make is a bid that tells partner that you have *at least an opening bid and good support for all three of the unbid suits.*

Well, there is just such a bid – the *take-out* or *informatory double.* Normally a double is used to suggest that you think that the opponents cannot make whatever contract they have got into; but there are few hands where, without having heard anything from your partner, you can be sure that the best thing to do is to try to punish your right-hand opponent at the One level. It is far more useful to use the double in this situation for showing the type of hand we have described above and asking partner to choose which of your three suits he prefers. Another point worth bearing in mind is that when the opponent's opening bid has been in one of the major suits, your take-out double suggests that you have at least four cards in the *other* major suit.

The example hand above is about minimum in terms of honour points for a take-out double. After all, it is a bid that requests partner to speak, even if he has a poor hand with very few points. This might mean that your side ends up playing the hand at the Two level with appreciably less than half the high cards in the pack. However, once partner has named a suit, you have good support for him and your hand will be increased in value because of your singleton. In an extreme case you might shade your point-count still more, but only with an especially suitable distribution, say:

♠ K Q 10 9 8
♥ —
♦ A 10 7 6
♣ K J 5 2

Here there are only 13 high card points, but the void in opponents' suit improves the hand more than the singleton.

Going the other way, towards a more balanced distribution, with:

♠ A Q 10 7
♥ 9 6 4
♦ A K 4
♣ K 3 2

you would still be worth a take-out double. The three small cards in the opposition suit are a defect when we are asking partner to bid another suit, but to offset that there are 16 high card points – probably a sensible minimum for a take-out double on such a balanced hand.

Now it is time to consider the situation from the other side of the table. Suppose the player on your left has opened One Spade, your partner has doubled, the next player has passed and you hold:

♠ 10 9 8
♥ 7 5 4 2
♦ 8 6 5
♣ 9 8 7

One thing is certain – you don't have to wait until you hold 6 points before you respond to a double, as you do after an ordinary opening bid. If you say No Bid in this position the contract will be One Spade doubled. You have no defence against this; your partner is probably short in spades, and the likely outcome is that the opposition will make One Spade doubled, perhaps with several overtricks. Letting the opponents make doubled overtricks is a very expensive hobby indeed. Think of it in this light: when your partner doubles, he is asking you a point-blank question to which he wants a reply. With the hand above, dreadful though it may be, you have no choice but to respond Two Hearts. Partner, remember, has better than a minimum opening and quite probably four hearts with you (he has doubled the other major).

There are two important points to stress at this stage:

1. You are only forced to reply to a take-out double with a terrible hand if the player on your right passes. If the bidding has gone South – One Spade, West – double, North – 1NT and you have the hand above, you could pass quite happily – the contract is no longer One Spade doubled, it is simply 1NT. Any advance in the auction automatically cancels the previous double. After the 1NT bid on your right, you would only make a bid if you held something worth telling partner about.

2. If you have doubled and, after a pass on your left, forced your partner to respond, then you must not get too excited. Just bear in mind what a depressing sort of hand you may have compelled him to bid on.

Cheer up! You won't always have hands like the one we have looked at. Suppose instead you had been dealt:

♠ 8 7
♥ K J 10 2
♦ A J 7 6
♣ 6 4 3

This is altogether more promising, with a full 9 points and a doubleton in spades as well. With a hand of 8–10 points you want to wake partner up to the idea that you have a fair hand, and the way to do this is to jump the bidding in your best suit. With this hand, bearing in mind that partner should have good support for the other major, you bid Three Hearts. This is an encouraging bid, but not forcing – if partner has nothing to spare for his double he can pass.

When you have an even stronger hand, one with 11 points or more, you want to be in game facing partner's better than minimum opening bid. If you have a long suit, you have no worries as to which game to choose. So with:

♠ 8
♥ K J 10 6 5 2
♦ A J 7 6
♣ 6 4

(9 high card points and 2 extra points for the long suit) you can jump straight to game in hearts. But with, say:

♠ 6 5 3
♥ K Q 7 2
♦ A Q 4 3
♣ Q 6

you cannot be quite sure that hearts is going to be the right contract and yet you want to assure partner that between you there are game-going values. The only completely forcing bid available to you is a bid in the opponents' suit! This is called a *cue-bid*. It is, of course, not made with the intention of playing in that suit but merely to insist on a game. So with the above hand you bid Two Spades and neither you nor partner can stop bidding until game is reached.

Sometimes you will hold a hand containing fair values in the suit that the opposition have bid. For example, after One Spade on your left and double from partner, you might hold:

♠ Q J 9 4
♥ Q 6 3
♦ J 7 4
♣ J 5 3

There is no temptation to invent a bid in clubs, diamonds or hearts.

Nor have you got sufficient values in spades to want to defend against a contract of One Spade doubled. The solution is to bid 1NT. Even if partner has a small singleton in spades you are prepared to play in no-trumps for, with the lead coming up to you, your holding in the suit should give you a double guard.

Equally, with:

```
♠ Q J 9 4
♥ A 6 3
♦ Q 7 4
♣ J 5 3
```

you would be worth a jump to 2NT. Of course, any shortage in spades that your partner might have will not be of any use in a no-trump contract – then the only things that bring in tricks are high-card points. With another point or so and a similar hand you could go all the way to 3NT in response to the double.

If you have fully absorbed the idea that you *must* respond to your partner's take-out double if there is a pass on your right, good, because now is the time to let you into a secret. You *can* pass your partner's double if you have a suitable hand. And a suitable hand is one that is *very strong and long in the opponents' suit, with good trick-taking potential.* If the opening bid is One Spade and you decide to pass the double for penalties, you are telling partner that your trump holding is very good indeed. So good, in fact, that you can stand a trump lead from him even if he has only a small singleton. By refusing to bid you will have converted partner's take-out double into a *penalty double* and you will be telling him that you expect to get rich on the proceeds.

Suppose you had been dealt:

```
♠ Q J 10 9 3 2
♥ 9
♦ A K 6
♣ 9 5 3
```

and partner doubled an opening bid of One Spade for take-out; you would be delighted to pass. Your hand is very rich in tricks if you are allowed to defend against a spade contract. In spades you have three tricks, very possibly four, and you have Ace and King of diamonds as well. What is more, partner has already told you that he has got an opening bid. You will be very disappointed if the contract of One Spade does not go three or four off. It is perfectly true that your side *may* have been able to make a game, but a bird in the hand . . .

There are three primary rules to remember if your partner has made a take-out double.

1. The weaker your hand, the more imperative it is for you to make a bid. You only pass for penalties when you are strong in the opponents' suit.

2. A jump bid in response to partner's double shows some values, perhaps 8–10 points, and is encouraging but not forcing.

3. The only 'forcing-to-game' bid, short of a direct jump to game if you are certain where you want to play the hand, is a cue-bid in the opponents' suit.

Beginners often get confused between penalty doubles (sometimes spoken of as *business* doubles) and the take-out doubles discussed above. So far we have only considered one situation – an immediate double of an opening bid. However, there is a little bit more to it than that. It can be a complicated business to decide exactly which double is for a take-out (even experts have been known to get this one wrong!), but a few rules and examples will go a long way towards clarifying the matter. A double is for take-out only if all three of these conditions are satisfied:

a The doubler's partner has not yet made a call, except possibly No Bid. So in the sequence:

South	*West*	*North*	*East*
NB	1♥	Dble	

the double is for take-out, but in:

South	*West*	*North*	*East*
1♣	1♥	Dble	

the double is for penalties. You could, after all, hardly be asking your partner what his best suit was – he has already told you! The double says that if South has a normal opening bid, North does not expect West to make seven tricks with hearts as trumps.

b The contract has not got to the Three level or higher. So after:

South	West	North	East
1♥	NB	2♥	Dble

East's double is for take-out, and if South passes West will be expected to take some action. However, if North had responded Four Hearts to his partner's opening and you held, perhaps:

♠ 6 4 2
♥ K Q J 10
♦ A 7 5 4
♣ A 9

you would certainly expect to beat this contract (you have three certain trump tricks and two Aces). Naturally enough, you would like to double and increase the penalty that your side is going to collect. But it would be infuriating if partner took the double as if for take-out and wandered off into Five Clubs or something equally unsuitable. Doubles at this level are always strictly for business.

c The contract is not a no-trump contract. Suppose you doubled an opening bid of 1NT by your right-hand opponent. Your partner could hardly expect you to hold good support for all four suits! A double of a no-trump contract is always purely for business and is usually based on a hand stronger than the opening 1NT bid. In effect you are saying that if the rest of the high cards of the pack are shared equally between your partner and the partner of the 1NT bidder, then your side will have the edge in points and you would expect 1NT to fail. If your partner doubles a no-trump contract by the opponents you are usually very pleased to pass – the stronger your hand the better, as the penalty will be larger. About your only excuse for removing the double would be if you held a very weak hand with a very long suit – useless in defence against 1NT, but capable of making tricks if you are allowed to play with your long suit as trumps.

Try to decide whether the doubles that follow are for take-out or business. The answers are at the end.

	South	West	North	East
a	1♦	NB	1♥	Dble

	South	West	North	East
b	1♦	3NT	Dble	

c	South	West	North	East
	1♥	1♠	NB	NB
	Dble			

d	South	West	North	East
	1♣	NB	1♥	NB
	1♠	Dble		

a. Take-out East is telling his partner that he has a better than minimum opening bid and that most of his values lie in the two unbid suits, clubs and spades. West is invited to bid either of these suits.

b. Penalties An easy one! Not only has partner bid, but the opponents are in no-trumps and they are up at the Three level.

c. Take-out South must have quite a bit to spare for his opening bid as, in spite of his partner's silence on the first round, he thinks that it is worth while fighting on. In addition to the heart suit that South has already mentioned, he is saying that he is quite happy with the idea of playing the hand in either diamonds or clubs as well.

d. Penalties More difficult, this one, and apparently an exception to the rules we started with. But with only one unbid suit, West could hardly be asking his partner to bid it – he could have done that himself over One Club if he had wanted to. The only explanation must be that West has good defence against a spade contract and perhaps does not expect the opposition to stay in spades.

MAKING A PRE-EMPTIVE BID

We have discussed jump overcalls earlier; when a player has a good but one-suited hand he can show where his values lie by making a bid one level higher than he normally would. For example, Two Spades over One Heart, or Three Diamonds over One Spade are strong jump overcalls. However, a pre-emptive bid is a call of more than one level higher than necessary, perhaps Three Spades over One Club, or Five Diamonds over One Spade. We will be discussing opening pre-emptive bids in more detail in the next chapter; suffice it to say that these overcalls have just the same purpose as the openings. They are designed, purely and simply, to annoy the opponents and make it difficult for them to reach their correct contract. They are based on a very long suit, of at least seven cards, and are not made when you have a good hand. One example, just to whet your appetite for the next chapter:

♠ K J 10 9 7 6 4
♥ 4
♦ Q J 9 7
♣ 2

Over an opening bid of One Club on your right, you would call Three Spades. You have little defence against any contract the opponents get to and your aim is to make it difficult for them to find out what their best contract is. In spite of your lack of points, nothing very terrible can happen to you in Three Spades, because of your length in the suit; with spades as trumps you can make tricks.

9.   Pre-emptive bidding

All the bids that have been discussed so far have been based on a nice, simple philosophy – you bid what you think you can make. However, there are a number of situations in bridge where a player deliberately 'bids to lose'. It sounds illogical, but the reasons behind it are best illustrated by an example. Suppose that there have been two No Bids up to you and at love all (that is with neither side vulnerable) you hold:

       ♠ Q J 10 9 8 6 5
       ♥ 8
       ♦ A 7 2
       ♣ 3 2

One thing is certain: with only 7 honour points and only one defensive trick (the Ace of diamonds) you don't want partner to get the impression that you have the values for an opening bid. However, there is a special bid to describe a hand such as the one above. It is known as a *pre-emptive bid*, or a *barrage bid*, and in this case it would be an opening of Three Spades. The argument behind such a seemingly wild flight of fancy is as follows: since your partner has passed and you hold a less than average hand (as far as honour points are concerned), you expect the opposition to hold the balance of points. They could easily hold enough between them to make a game or even a slam. However, and this is the important point, in spite of the weakness of your hand you can make a lot of tricks if you are allowed to play with spades as trumps. Even if your partner has a completely hopeless collection of cards, you can still come to five tricks in spades and the Ace of diamonds.

Suppose the worst happens: you are doubled in a pre-emptive call of this nature and find partner with next to nothing. You can be 100% sure that the opposition have the strength to make at least game. By opening with a pre-empt you have thrown a spanner in the works as far as the opponents' bidding is concerned – you have raised a barrage. They will have to start their bidding at the Three or Four level and will find it difficult (and sometimes impossible) to arrive at the right contract. Even if they get the suit right, they may not be able to judge the correct level accurately.

However, the number of tricks that you can make if you are left to play in your pre-emptive call is important – you should reckon on losing not more than 500 points if you find your partner with nothing. This principle is usually referred to as the *Rule of Two and Three*.

As you can afford to lose 500 points, this means that if your side is vulnerable you don't mind going down two tricks doubled (losing 500 points), while if you are not vulnerable you can be more expensive and can risk a three tricks doubled defeat (again losing 500 points). You don't have to wait until your partner has passed before you make a bid like this – you can pre-empt as dealer or after a pass on your right. (There is little point in opening with a Three-bid after three passes – the best way to shut the opponents out will be to throw the hand in!)

So the hand we started considering:

♠ Q J 10 9 8 6 5
♥ 8
♦ A 7 2
♣ 3 2

qualifies for a non-vulnerable opening bid of Three Spades in first, second or third position – you expect to make six tricks with spades as trumps, three short of target. Looking on the bright side, even if partner has no high-card points, he may still have some values for you. Suppose you found him with:

♠ 7 4 3 2
♥ 5 4 3 2
♦ 3
♣ 7 6 5 4

a terrible hand at first sight, but just look at the tricks he is able to supply in a spade contract. Between the two hands you have eleven cards in spades, leaving only two for the opposition – the Ace and the King. If they hold one of these cards each, both of their spade winners will fall together as soon as you lead the suit. As far as the rest of the hand is concerned there are only two losers in clubs and one in hearts. Note how useful partner's singleton in diamonds will be – it means that you can trump twice in his hand. That will be four losers in all and you will end by actually making Three Spades. Even if you find one opponent with both the Ace and King of spades, there will still be only five losers and you will escape with a one-trick defeat.

Of course, your opponents are most unlikely to let you play in Three Spades. They have, after all, 33 high card points between them. But, it must be stressed again, you did not *expect* to play in Three Spades when you opened with your pre-empt. The other side will have had to start their bidding at the Four level, and may easily get things muddled. It is often hard enough, as you will appreciate by now, to get to the right contract if you have been given a clear run. Just think of the problems if you have been deprived of three whole rounds of bidding! A few more examples of pre-emptive openings are:

♠ 3
♥ K Q J 9 8 6 5 3
♦ J 10 6
♣ 4

With seven playing tricks in hearts you would, if not vulnerable, open Four Hearts; if vulnerable Three Hearts would be enough.

♠ 3
♥ A K Q J 8 7 6 4
♦ J 10 6
♣ 4

Now, with eight sure tricks in hearts, Four Hearts is the correct opening irrespective of the vulnerability.

♠ 3
♥ J 10 6
♦ A K Q J 8 7 6 4
♣ 4

Non-vulnerable, Five Diamonds is the recommended opening but vulnerable you would content yourself with Four Diamonds.

Note that with the last two examples it could be argued that you had enough honour points for an opening bid of One of your long suit. True, but you have virtually no defensive tricks against any contract that your opponents may play in. With an eight-card suit it is a bit much to expect both opponents to follow suit twice! Indeed, one of them may easily be void; then you will have no defence whatsoever. A far more practical approach, with these extremely one-suited hands lacking high cards outside the long suit, is to rush the bidding as much as possible.

There are several ways in which you can use these pre-emptive bids – as opening bids, as overcalls after the opponents have opened, and in response to an opening bid from your own partner. Remember, though, that when you *overcall*, a pre-emptive bid is at least two levels higher than a simple overcall. Thus East – One Club, South – Three Hearts is a pre-empt, but East – One Heart, South – Three Clubs is a single jump overcall of the type discussed in the last chapter and so shows a strong hand. Before you could pre-empt in clubs over a One Heart opening you would have to bid at least Four Clubs.

Care should also be taken when making a pre-empt after your partner has opened the bidding. Again your bid has to be at least two levels higher than a simple response, for a single jump in a new suit (such as South – One Heart, North – Three Clubs) is, as we have seen, a sign of great strength. Furthermore, there is much less reason for you to worry about what the opposition might be able to make if you have the assurance that your partner has an opening bid. But with, say:

♠ K Q J 10 8 7 4 3
♥ 6 5
♦ 4 2
♣ 8

it would be perfectly sensible to go straight to Four Spades over any opening bid partner makes. Whatever his hand, you can be pretty sure that Four Spades is going to be the right contract, and the easiest way of getting there is to bid it at once. The only difference between this sort of pre-empt and an opening bid of Three or Four is that now you expect to make your contract, as partner should be able to supply the three tricks that you will need.

A fundamental principle of sensible bidding is that when you have a strong hand with plenty of tricks you have no reason to fear any opposition bidding; your main aim in life is to take things quietly and leave plenty of room to discover whether you want to play in a slam, a game, or even a part-score if partner has very little. But with a weak, one-suited hand you can describe your holding in one bid and make the opponents' lives a misery into the bargain.

FACING A PRE-EMPTING PARTNER

Even if your partner has a strong hand, an opening pre-empt from you should not make things too difficult for him as he will know exactly what type of hand you have as well as how many playing tricks you are promising to provide in your suit. Nevertheless, there are a few points that are worth remembering when you find yourself facing a pre-empting partner.

First and foremost, don't get excited just because you hold a couple of Aces and the odd King. You must allow for the fact that your partner is *expecting* to go two or three down, according to the vulnerability – he will probably need your high cards to make his contract.

So, over a non-vulnerable opening of Three Spades you would pass with:

♠ A 6
♥ A 7 6 3
♦ K 10 7 4
♣ 8 6 4

but you would be prepared to go on to Four Spades if you had:

♠ A 6
♥ A K 7 6
♦ K Q 10 7
♣ 8 6 4

It is worth bearing in mind, when considering a raise of partner's pre-empt, that Aces and Kings (*quick* tricks) are far more likely to be of use to him than the same number of honour points made up by Queens and Jacks.

Second, don't be tempted to try your luck in no-trumps with a good hand just because you are short in your partner's suit. If he has a good suit, such as the seven card suits we have been considering as suitable for pre-emptive bids, he won't need any support as far as trumps are concerned. Just consider the following pair of hands:

West	East
♠ 4	♠ K Q J 10 9 8 7
♥ A K 5 4	♥ 7 3
♦ A 10 7 4	♦ 8
♣ A J 9 3	♣ 6 4 2

East has a reasonable non-vulnerable opening bid of Three Spades. Now if West foolishly tried 3NT, East (if he were a well disciplined player) would simply pass. In the play, East's spade suit would simply not feature at all and West would be restricted to four or five tricks. But if West had, far more sensibly, just raised Three Spades to Four Spades then East would have absolutely no problems whatsoever in the play. He would lose a spade trick and perhaps two club tricks to make his contract with great ease.

It may sound odd, but the fewer cards that you have in the suit in which partner has pre-empted, the more you want to play with his suit as trumps! It is only when you have a good fit in his suit, and *know that you will be able to use it*, that you should be tempted to try no-trumps. Consider this pair of hands:

West	East
♠ Q J 3	♠ 6 4
♥ A K 5 3	♥ 8 2
♦ K Q 7	♦ 6 3
♣ K 7 5	♣ A Q J 10 9 6 3

Suppose East opens Three Clubs; now is the time for West, with an excellent fit for clubs in the shape of ♣K 7 5 to try 3NT. It is worth noting that game in East's suit (Five Clubs) has no chance whatsoever – there are three top losers – but 3NT cannot possibly be defeated.

Third, if you do bid a new suit in reply to a pre-empt by your partner, this is forcing to game and partner, no matter how weak his pre-empt, will be forced to bid on. So one thing is clear; you don't introduce an indifferent suit of your own just because you don't care much for partner's – almost inevitably you will do better to choose between raising partner and saying No Bid.

If the opponents join in over a pre-empt from your partner, there are basically three things that you can do. Suppose partner has opened Three Spades and your right-hand opponent has found a bid of Four Hearts. You could:

a. Support partner If you were planning to bid game anyhow, irrespective of the intervention, there is no reason to hold back; but with a hand such as:

♠ A 6 3
♥ 8 7
♦ K Q 6 3
♣ J 10 5 2

it would be reasonable to judge that the opposition could make their contract of Four Hearts. On the other hand, it looks as though you have two tricks in support of your partner in a spade contract and, although you would have been content to pass Three Spades if your opponents had kept quiet, it would be sensible now to try Four Spades. This is a contract that you do not expect to fail by more than one or two tricks and which should prove a cheap save against the game which the opposition have reached. On your lucky days, they won't be content with a small penalty and may go on to Five Hearts. Then, if they come to only ten tricks, your little push will have paid handsome dividends.

b. Double for penalties With a hand such as:

♠ 2
♥ K J 9 4
♦ K Q 10 5
♣ A J 9 6

you would be right to judge that the opponents were out of their depth. In spite of the fact that your partner has warned you that he has one defensive trick at most, you have good grounds for supposing that the opposition cannot make Four Hearts, or indeed any other contract. A double would be correct and you would be equally happy to get to work on Five Diamonds or Five Clubs if they decided to change their ground.

A word of warning for the player who has made a pre-emptive bid: if his partner subsequently doubles the other side, the last thing that is required is another call from the pre-empter. Remember, by pre-empting you have not guaranteed a single defensive trick; if partner does decide to double, that is entirely his own affair – he is not expecting anything in the way of defence in your hand.

c. Pass, and hope that the opponents are in the wrong contract With:

♠ 3 2
♥ K J 9 4
♦ 6 5 3
♣ A 8 7 2

you would simply hope that the opposition stopped at Four Hearts – a contract that you suspect will fail. It would be a mistake, however, to double, for they might try their luck in Five Diamonds and against that contract your side has very little defence. Be content that your partner's pre-empt has rushed the opponents into what appears to be the wrong contract.

A final cautionary note for the player who has made a pre-emptive bid: once you have made your bid, unless partner forces you to go on by responding in a new suit below the game level, you never, never bid again. Partner knows exactly what you have got; you don't know what he has got.

RESPONDING TO OPPONENTS' PRE-EMPT

We have spent some time discussing pre-emptive bidding from the angle of the side which has made the pre-empt. Naturally enough, there is another important question to be considered: what do you do if the opponents pre-empt against you? A lot of the time, of course, you will have little choice but to say No Bid. Joining in will commit your side to playing at the Three or Four level and if you have heard nothing from your partner you need a pretty strong hand to take that risk.

If you have a reasonably good one-suited hand, you have to take a chance and plunge into the auction in case your side is being talked out of an easy game or even a slam. But you will do so with your heart in your mouth – if most of the outstanding strength lies with the pre-empter's partner you may be inviting a crushing penalty double.

Over a pre-empt at the Four or the Five level you simply have to use your own judgement, but over opening Three-bids there are several conventional bids that can be arranged. It will be sensible to mention the two most popular which are '3NT for take-out' and 'Lower Minor'. Which you decide to play is something that you must discuss with your partner when you sit down at the table. It would be nice not to have to make up your mind until the hand turned up, but the rules of the game don't allow any discussion of your bidding methods once you have looked at your hand! Both of these conventions are for take-out – just like the informatory or take-out double that was considered in the last chapter.

If you have arranged to play 3NT for take-out over opening Three level pre-empts by the opposition, the bid simply asks partner to bid his best suit. With a three-suited hand such as:

♠ 2
♥ K Q J 4
♦ A Q J 5
♣ A J 10 8

you would be prepared to take the risk of joining in if you were faced with an opening bid of Three Spades on your right. Bidding 3NT to ask partner which of the three unbid suits he prefers is a lot more flexible than taking a wild guess as to which suit to bid. Naturally enough, you need a good hand (certainly no weaker than the one above) for partner is forced to speak at the Four level. This method has one big drawback: if you think that you can make nine tricks in no-trumps, you will have to think twice about bidding 3NT over a Three-bid, for partner is almost sure to respond and dutifully tell you about his best suit! Nevertheless, this 3NT convention is perhaps the most popular way of combating Three-bids.

If, instead, your side had agreed to play the Lower Minor convention, this would mean that over an opening bid of Three Clubs a bid of Three Diamonds from you would be asking for partner's best suit, while over an opening of Three Diamonds, Three Hearts, or Three Spades your bid for a take-out would be Four Clubs. This idea has some advantages over the 3NT method – over an opening Three Clubs by the opposition you can sometimes buy the contract at the Three level instead of the Four level, and you are able to bid 3NT if that is where you want to play. However, every method has its built-in drawbacks. If you play Lower Minor you will find it difficult to take action over Three Clubs if you hold, say:

♠ 7
♥ A J 4
♦ A K Q 10 9 7 6
♣ 8 3

for if you bid Three Diamonds, your partner is sure to launch into Three Spades or something equally unsuitable!

If it weren't so difficult to combat, the idea of opening Three of a suit would have gone out of fashion years ago!

The following hand is a good example of Three-bids in action at the table:

Dealer, South   Love all

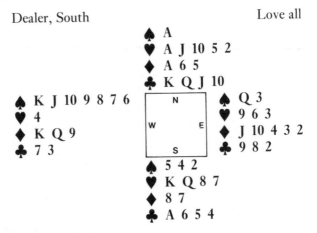

This was the bidding:

South	West	North	East
NB	3♠ *a*	4♣ *b*	NB
4♥ *c*	NB *d*	NB *e*	NB

a. A typical opening Three Spades bid. West had only 9 honour points and one defensive trick outside the spade suit. He could at most lose two tricks in the spade suit, and so have five spade tricks and a trick in diamonds – six tricks in all. So, not vulnerable, the worst that could happen if he found partner with absolute rubbish was to go three off for a penalty of 500 points.

b. North-South had arranged to play Lower Minor for take-out. Although the North hand is not ideal, some action had to be taken, and North consoled himself with the thought that if partner bid Four Diamonds it would be possible to go to hearts without increasing the level. A possible alternative was to double Three Spades for penalties, but North could not be sure of defeating this contract. Even if it went one off, that would be a poor return if North-South could make a game.

c. South knew that his partner had support for hearts, the other major, but in bidding Four Hearts he was conscious of making something of an underbid – after all he might have been forced to respond with no points at all, and he has 9 honour points. Five Hearts was a possible bid, but South argued that his partner may have taken something of a chance in getting into the bidding and it would be foolish to go to Five and go off, when stopping in Four would have led to an easy game. He consoled himself with the thought that if the opposition fought on to Four Spades, he would be able to show his other suit with a bid of Five Clubs.

d. Once a player has made a pre-emptive bid, the golden rule is that he never speaks again in the auction – partner is in charge.

e. No reason to go on, as partner might have no points at all.

There was very little of interest in the play. West chose to lead a club and after winning declarer drew trumps in three rounds. He eventually gave up a diamond trick, trumped a diamond in his own hand and had twelve tricks, made up of four clubs, five hearts, one ruff in hand, and the Aces of spades and diamonds. This was a typical triumph for a pre-empt. East-West lost points on the deal when their opponents made a game, but the Three Spades bid made it very difficult for them to find out that Six Hearts would have been a good contract. Given a free run, they might easily have reached Six Hearts (or Six Clubs, which is just as good) and would then have scored not only the game but the bonus of 500 points for bidding and making a slam. On this occasion the pre-empt saved 500 points; at the same time it risked little. For suppose West had had to play in Three Spades: only in North-South had found the perfect defence could they have held him to seven tricks. More likely he would have been allowed to make eight to go one off only – a worthwhile investment.

10. Forcing bids and other strong openings

Every once in a while (but not nearly often enough!) you will get dealt an enormously strong hand. It will be necessary to make an opening bid that either tells partner that you are good enough for game on your own or, possibly, that you are prepared to play in game if partner has a few 'bits and pieces', perhaps not enough to respond to an ordinary opening bid of One of a suit.

There are three strong opening bids that you can use, depending upon the type and strength of your hand:

1. Two Clubs – forcing to game – a conventional bid.
2. Two of any other suit – very strong – natural (you have the suit that you bid) – not insisting on game.
3. Two No-trumps – a very strong balanced hand, but again not insisting on game.

Let's consider these possibilities in order:

TWO CLUBS

A player who opens the bidding with Two Clubs is alerting his partner to the fact that he wants to play in a game, no matter how bad the responder's hand might be. The bid is conventional (as was the Stayman convention that you met before) and bears no relation whatsoever to the club holding. A player who has started the auction with Two Clubs may turn out to have a singleton in the suit, or even a void. Equally, it is possible that he may turn up with a long club suit – only the subsequent action will reveal his hand. Note that it is only the *opening* bid of Two Clubs that is conventional. If your partner opens the bidding with One Spade and you *respond* Two Clubs you are simply showing a fair club suit and at least 8 points; if your right-hand opponent opens the bidding and you *overcall* with Two Clubs, you are not showing anything special –

just a good club suit. Only when Two Clubs is the first bid of the auction (other than preceding No Bids) is it conventional.

To say that the bid is 'forcing to game' means that neither his partner nor the player who has opened Two Clubs can stop bidding until at least a game has been reached. Sometimes, of course, the opening bid may be a prelude to better things: the partnership may go on to a small slam (twelve tricks) or even a grand slam (all thirteen tricks), but slam bidding will be considered in more detail in the next chapter.

Just consider a hand like this:

♠ A K
♥ A K Q 4
♦ A Q J 10
♣ A Q 8

You have 29 honour points and, if you played in a no-trump contract, nine absolutely certain tricks, even if partner hasn't got a single point in his hand. (After, say, a spade lead you simply lead diamonds until someone takes his King and then you will have two spades, three hearts, three diamonds and a club for your contract.) However, you need so little from partner in the way of points or distribution that you would not be satisfied with a contract of 3NT until you had explored the possibilities of a slam in either hearts or diamonds. Just suppose that these were the two hands:

♠ A K   ♠ 9 8 7
♥ A K Q 4   ♥ 6 5 3
♦ A Q J 10   ♦ 9 8 7 4 3 2
♣ A Q 8   ♣ 4

Partner has not got a solitary point, but what a marvelous fit if the hands are played with diamonds as trumps. There are no spade losers, as you can trump the third spade in your hand, no heart or club losers because partner's trumps can take care of your low cards in these suits, and all you might lose is one trick to the King of diamonds. A small slam is virtually a 'lay-down' – an expression often used by bridge players to describe a contract that does not require any deep thought. To give your side a chance of reaching a successful slam in diamonds you do not open 3NT, but start off with Two Clubs and give partner a chance to tell you what he has. Remember, if you start with Two Clubs there is no danger of partner drying up on you – he is committed, like you, to continue bidding until a game is reached.

To open Two Clubs you need at least 23 honour points. You may think that this number of points is a little odd, bearing in mind that a partnership should normally share 26 points before going on to game. But rest assured, this apparent anomaly will be explained in due course.

Consider another strong hand:

♠ A K Q 8 7
♥ A K Q 6 3
♦ 9
♣ A J

You would be very unlucky not to take ten or eleven tricks with either major suit as trumps, even if partner held:

♠ 6 5 3
♥ 5 4 2
♦ 6 5 3 2
♣ 8 6 5

or something equally depressing, you would be quite happy with the prospects of making game. But it would be foolish to *guess* in which suit you wanted to play – partner could hold one of these two hands:

♠ 10 9 6 4 3   ♠ 2
♥ 2   ♥ 10 9 7 4 2
♦ 8 7 6 5   ♦ 8 7 6 5
♣ 4 3 2   ♣ 4 3 2

in which case Four Spades would be easy on the first hand but Four Hearts might fail, while exactly the opposite would apply if he held the second hand. The idea here is to open Two Clubs to establish a forcing to game situation. Then, with no sense of urgency, you can bid both of your suits and see which one partner prefers.

Now, what of the poor partner of the Two Clubs bidder? So far he has only been allowed to hold some pretty depressing hands, and yet he must find a bid to keep the auction alive until a game is reached. To show the sort of hand on which you would not have spoken at all if partner had merely opened with a One-bid, you have a special, conventional reply: Two Diamonds. In the same way that Two Clubs bears no relation to the opener's club suit, so a response of Two Diamonds has nothing to do with a diamond suit. It is referred to as a *negative response*.

As you might guess, if there is a negative response to Two Clubs, there is sure to be a positive response of some sort. And positive responses to Two Clubs are completely natural – if you respond Two Spades, it is because you have a spade suit and so on. It is only the negative Two Diamonds bid that is conventional or artificial.

Before you can give a positive reply, you need a certain minimum of high cards. And these high-card requirements cannot be measured in terms of honour points – it is the responder's ability to take *quick tricks* that determines whether or not he is worth a positive response. You should work on this scale:

Ace and King in the same suit	2 quick tricks
Ace	1 quick trick
King and Queen in the same suit	1 quick trick
King (protected with at least one low card)	$\frac{1}{2}$ quick trick

A positive response to Two Clubs absolutely guarantees at least one and a half quick tricks. With less than one and a half, you have to content yourself with a negative Two Diamonds.

Imagine that your partner has opened Two Clubs. Consider a few possible responding hands:

a

♠ 5 3
♥ K 10 7 4 2
♦ 9 8 6
♣ A 3 2

The Ace of clubs is one quick trick, the King of hearts is half a quick trick, so with the required one and a half quick tricks you are worth a positive response. You have a biddable heart suit, so there is no real problem in choosing the correct reply of Two Hearts.

b

♠ 5 3
♥ 9 8 6
♦ K 10 7 4 2
♣ A 3 2

Again the hand contains the required one and a half quick tricks, but just stop to think for a moment! You can't bid Two Diamonds, for that is the conventional bid that we have set aside for a negative response. The solution is not too difficult: you must bid Three Diamonds to show a positive response with a diamond suit.

c

♠ 4
♥ K Q J 10 7 6 4
♦ 8 4 3
♣ 10 5

Careful! Were you thinking of showing that magnificent heart suit? You can't do that yet, because you have not got the required one and a half quick tricks. You must content yourself with Two Diamonds to start with, and tell your partner about the hearts later. The danger is that he might have a hand such as:

♠ K Q J 10 9 8 6
♥ A 2
♦ A K
♣ A K

If you had responded Two Hearts he would know that you held ♠A and ♥K – that would be the only way to make up one and a half quick tricks. To save time he would simply bid Seven Spades or Seven No-trumps, and that would be a disaster as your side is missing the Ace of spades!

d

♠ Q J 4
♥ K 8 6
♦ 9 5 3 2
♣ K 7 4

This is a different type of hand to the ones above and serves to introduce a rather special type of positive response. Indeed, some players give it a special name and refer to it as a *semi-positive response*. The best way to describe your holding is to respond 2NT. This shows a minimum of 8 honour points, no biddable suit, and a reasonably balanced hand.

So your possible responses to Two Clubs are as follows:

Two Spades, Two Hearts, Three Diamonds, Three Clubs – positive responses showing a biddable suit and at least one and a half quick tricks.

Two No-trumps – positive response showing at least 8 points and a balanced hand.

Two Diamonds – negative response, denying the qualifications for a positive.

We started this discussion on the Two Clubs opening bid by saying that it totally committed the partnership to game. Unfortunately bridge is a game where you never say 'never' and you never say 'always'. It is time to let you into another secret: there are two situations where the opening allows the bidding to stop short of the game level. Let's consider the commoner case first. Suppose that you had been dealt:

♠ K Q 4
♥ A K 7
♦ A K J 10
♣ K 10 2

Certainly, with 23 honour points, your hand qualifies for a Two Clubs opening. But where are you going for game if partner has a poor hand, with no long suit? The solution is to open Two Clubs but, after partner's response, rebid 2NT. This shows a balanced hand and tells partner that you hold precisely 23 or 24 points. Furthermore, if the responder holds less than 3 points and no long suit, he is at liberty to pass. So, if these were the two hands:

West	*East*
♠ K Q 4	♠ J 7 2
♥ A K 7	♥ 8 5 3 2
♦ A K J 10	♦ 9 7
♣ K 10 2	♣ J 6 5 3

the bidding would go West – Two Clubs, East – Two Diamonds, West – 2NT, East – No Bid. Looking at the two hands together there should be two tricks in spades, two in hearts, at least three in diamonds, and one in clubs. Together they have a good chance of making 2NT but, short of miracles, 3NT will not be made.

Just suppose that opener's hand had been improved a little to become:

♠ K Q 4
♥ A K 7
♦ A K J 10
♣ K Q 10

Now he has 25 honour points and is too good for the non-forcing rebid of 2NT over the negative Two Diamonds. The solution would be to rebid 3NT as, no matter how bad responder's hand may be, the opener is prepared to have a go at game.

However, if you and your partner have been given a free run in the bidding, it is only the sequence Two Clubs, Two Diamonds (negative), 2NT that allows you to stop short of game. If your rebid had been any suit call, your partner would know that you did not hold this balanced type of hand with 23–24 points and would be compelled to go on bidding until a game was reached.

Note the condition in the last paragraph, 'if you and your partner have been given a free run'. This gives a clue as to the other set of circumstances in which the Two Club bidder and his partner can stop short of a game. If the opponents join in the bidding, it may well prove to be more profitable to double them for a large penalty rather than go for a game. However, you should be sure that it is going to be a *worthwhile* penalty. There is little point in doubling to collect a paltry 100 or 300 points if your side can make a comfortable game – that would be a worthwhile sacrifice for them!

TWO OF ANY OTHER SUIT

There is a very big difference between hands that qualify for an opening Two Clubs and the common or garden opening bids that have been considered earlier on. In the gap between come all those hands that are prepared to have a shot at game if partner has perhaps one or two useful cards, and yet may be passed out if you open with only one of your suit as partner may lack the 6 points that he needs to respond.

Look at this hand:

♠ A K Q 10 9 5
♥ A Q 7
♦ A 6 3
♣ 2

and suppose that partner has one of the following hands:

	a		*b*
♠	8 7 5	♠	8 7 5
♥	4 3 2	♥	4 3
♦	7 5 4 2	♦	K 5 4 2
♣	10 9 5	♣	10 9 5 3

If you open Two Clubs and find partner with *a*, you will inevitably get too high – there are at least four certain losers with spades as trumps. But if you decide to open One Spade, you may find partner with hand *b*. Without the 6 points that he needs to respond, you will find yourself left in One Spade. And yet the bits and pieces that hand *b* can provide are all that you need to make game in spades. It has three real assets – three trumps, a useful doubleton in hearts, and the King of diamonds, and ten tricks for game in spades will be straightforward.

The solution is to open with a Two-bid in Spades. Opening Twos in suits other than clubs (which, as we have seen, are set aside for a special purpose) are natural bids, showing the suit named, and are forcing for at least one round (partner must make at least one bid in reply). Again, the opening bid is rather specialized. Before you open with a Two-bid you should have at least *six cards* in the suit. You should have a self-sufficient suit with, generally speaking, *not more than one loser*. You should also have a hand that *expects to win at least eight tricks*, even if partner has nothing, and it should contain *at least four defensive tricks*. A defensive trick is really the same thing as our old friend, the quick trick.

These are some typical opening Two-bids:

Hand a

♠ A K J 10 5 3
♥ A K
♦ A 3 2
♣ 7 6

Hand b

♠ A 7
♥ A 2
♦ A K Q J 10 4
♣ 9 5 3

Hand c

♠ 8 5
♥ A K Q 7 5 4
♦ A K J 6
♣ 2

Hand d

♠ K Q J 10 8 6
♥ K Q 2
♦ A K
♣ 7 5

Hand a contains five defensive tricks (♠A K, ♥A K, ♦A). The spade suit is almost sure to provide five tricks (one may be lost to the missing Queen), so the hand should be worth eight tricks. *Hand b* has got ♠A, ♥A and ♦A K for its defensive tricks, and has certainly got eight sure winners. *Hand c* is a little more border-line – there are the necessary defensive tricks and the good six-card suit, but you can't be quite sure about eight winners. Nevertheless, Two Hearts would be the best practical opening bid. With *Hand d* there is no difficulty in deciding on Two Spades as the right opening – it has all the necessary qualifications.

Now, what about responding if your partner has opened with a Two-bid in a suit other than clubs? Remember, his bid is forcing for at least one round, so even with a completely useless collection of cards you have to keep the bidding alive. In the same way that there is a negative response to an opening Two Clubs (that is, Two Diamonds), so there is an artificial negative response to these other Two-bids. It is 2NT. It does not suggest that you want to play the hand in no-trumps; merely that you have a poor hand.

You know that partner has something like eight or nine tricks in his own hand (with ten, he would probably have opened Two Clubs so as to be sure of ending in game), so you do not need a great deal of encouragement to go on after hearing a Two-bid from him. If you have got a trick and a half for him, or perhaps eight or nine points, you are worth a positive response. This can take the form of supporting partner's suit or showing a suit of your own, and once you have shown a hand with these values neither of the partners can (or would want to!) stop bidding short of game. One important thought is that although you normally do not support your partner after a One-bid unless you have four or more cards in his suit (as the opening bid may be based on only a four-card suit), the situation is a little different if he has promised a good six-card suit or better. You no longer have to wait for four-card support before you raise him – three low cards or even a doubleton honour will usually be quite sufficient support. It is usually a mistake to tell him about a moth-eaten suit of your own if you are quite happy with his suit. For example, with:

♠ A 6 4
♥ K 5 3
♦ J 8 4 3 2
♣ 7 4

you should not be tempted to show your bad diamonds over an opening of Two Spades or Two Hearts – it would be far better to support partner's suit immediately.

To sum up, from the responder's point of view: with a worthless responding hand you start with the negative 2NT and plan to pass on the next round if all the opener can do is rebid his original suit at the lowest level; with perhaps one trick to help partner you start with the negative response but then go on to game after partner's rebid; with a trick and a half or better you start with the positive response.

Finally, we have to consider further action by the opening bidder. Suppose you have opened with a Two-bid (other than Two Clubs) and have received a positive response from partner: you have no real problems, as both members of the partnership know that they hold enough for game. You will carry on quietly describing your hand – showing another suit if you have one, supporting partner's suit if you can, or rebidding your own long suit. However, after a negative 2NT from partner you must proceed with a certain amount of caution, for it is quite possible that partner has nothing to offer. Take the four example hands that we started with and suppose partner has responded 2NT to your opening Two-bid. You would rebid as follows:

Hand a Three Spades. You have nothing to spare for your opening bid and any further effort must come from partner. If he has, perhaps, the Ace of clubs and three small spades he will raise

Three Spades to Four – a contract that would be quite reasonable.

Hand b 3NT. Something of a gamble (partner might be very poor) but you have eight absolutely certain winners in your hand and almost anything that partner can provide may give a ninth trick. You would be very unlucky to go more than one off. Note that we try for game in no-trumps on this hand. It is the old story: game in no-trumps only requires nine tricks, but game in diamonds needs eleven.

Hand c Three Diamonds. It is usually more sensible to show a second suit if it is of good quality. However, if partner can only give simple preference to Three Hearts, you should pass on the next round. If he had values that were likely to be useful to you he could have given jump preference by calling Four Hearts – you wouldn't get too excited by that, as he had started by giving the negative 2NT, denying much in the way of high cards.

Hand d Three Spades. Again you have little to spare for your opening and must give partner room to pass if he is poor.

TWO NO-TRUMPS

The third type of opening Two-bid is an opening of 2NT. Just like any other no-trump bid it shows a balanced hand (no long suits, no short suits, high cards well shared out) and this time promises 20–22 points. They will all be high-card points – you shouldn't have a distributional hand if you are thinking of bidding no-trumps, and distributional points are no use in no-trump contracts anyway. It is not forcing. Partner without a long suit will pass unless he holds four or five points, in which case he will have quite enough to go on to a game. Some typical 2NT openers would be:

♠ A K 7 3
♥ Q J 10
♦ K 7 6
♣ A K J

perfect for no-trumps with the 4–3–3–3 distribution, and ideal for 2NT with 21 honour points. Or:

♠ A Q 2
♥ A K
♦ A Q 8
♣ J 8 6 4 2

Here there are 20 points in high cards and also a five-card suit, perhaps not so usual for a no-trump bid. However, it is not a particularly strong five-card suit, and to open One Club instead might run a very real risk of missing a good game if you found partner with 5 points. Again:

♠ Q J 6
♥ A K 9 4 2
♦ A Q J
♣ A J

This would be an absolute maximum for an opening of 2NT. With another odd Jack in the hand you would open Two Clubs and plan to rebid 2NT (showing, if you remember, 23–24 points). However, you are much too good with the actual hand to open One Heart and your heart suit is not good enough to contemplate an opening Two-bid in the suit.

Responding to 2NT is an easy affair – after all, partner's opening bid has told you to within a point how strong he is and you have a good idea of his distribution as well. As already mentioned, with less than 5 points and a balanced hand you simply pass. However, an important difference between responding to 2NT and responding to 1NT is that you do not have so much room to manoeuvre over 2NT. Over 1NT you had two bids available to tell partner that you did not like his suggestion of no-trumps – you could bid Two of a suit (the weak take-out) warning him to pass; or you could bid Three of a suit to tell him that in spite of your dislike of no-trumps you wanted to end up in game. Over 2NT there is the simple arrangement that *any response (other than No Bid) is forcing to game.* If you are happy enough with partner's suggestion of no-trumps and have enough points for game, just raise to 3NT. But if you have the values for game and yet think that the hand would be better played in a suit, all you need do is bid Three of that suit. This is forcing (partner must bid again), and you can find out whether he likes your suit.

To call a suit, so suggesting a dislike of no-trumps, you must have *at least a five-card suit*. Take this hand:

♠ 8 5
♥ K J 10 7 4
♦ 6 3
♣ K Q 3 2

and suppose that partner has opened 2NT. It could be that he has a slight weakness in either spades or diamonds (suits where you hold only a low doubleton) and that Four Hearts will be a better and safer contract. So the best bid is Three Hearts. Partner will know that you have at least five cards in the suit and will raise to Four Hearts if he has three or more hearts in his hand. With only a doubleton heart he will rebid 3NT, and then you will have to take a slight chance on the weak suits. However, it will have cost you nothing to try, and may gain handsomely.

But with this hand:

♠ 8
♥ J 10 7 6 5
♦ 6 3 2
♣ 10 9 3 2

although you are not pleased with the idea of no-trumps, there is little that you can do about it, for any bid by you will not be passed by the opener and your side is bound to get too high. All that you can do is to pass the 2NT bid and cross your fingers!

Finally, over a 2NT opening bid the responder can use the Stayman convention that we met in reply to 1NT. Perhaps it's not quite the same, for then the conventional bid was Two Clubs. Here, after 2NT, Three Clubs is the bid that asks the opening bidder if he has a four-card major. If he has, he bids it; but lacking four cards in either spades or hearts he replies Three Diamonds. The convention would pay off on these hands:

West	*East*
♠ A K 7 3	♠ Q J 6 4
♥ Q J 10	♥ 3
♦ K 7 6	♦ Q J 10 9 4
♣ A K J	♣ Q 4 2

After West has opened 2NT, East with 8 high-card points has the values for game. Without the aid of the Stayman convention he would probably go straight to game in no-trumps without showing his diamond suit. (East would be more interested in the nine-trick game in no-trumps than in the eleven-trick game in diamonds.) If the hands were played in 3NT, West would be in trouble after the likely heart lead. He has only one guard in the suit and this would be knocked out at once. Then there would be no way of coming to nine tricks without playing on the diamond suit, and as soon as the suit was led the opposition would jump in with their Ace and take enough heart tricks to defeat the contract. However, if East had used the Stayman Three Clubs bid over the opening, asking for major suits, he could have hit the bull's-eye. West would respond Three Spades and East could go to Four Spades, secure in the knowledge that the partnership held eight spades between them. With spades as trumps, there should be a safe and easy play for eleven tricks; declarer loses only to the Ace of diamonds and a top heart, as dummy's singleton heart prevents the loss of more than one trick in the suit.

To conclude, consider a full hand illustrating a Two-bid in action. There is also an interesting point or two in the play, in case you are getting bored with bidding!

Dealer, East   Love all

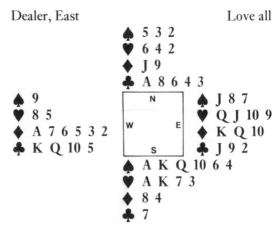

```
                    ♠ 5 3 2
                    ♥ 6 4 2
                    ♦ J 9
                    ♣ A 8 6 4 3
   ♠ 9                              ♠ J 8 7
   ♥ 8 5                            ♥ Q J 10 9
   ♦ A 7 6 5 3 2                    ♦ K Q 10
   ♣ K Q 10 5                       ♣ J 9 2
                    ♠ A K Q 10 6 4
                    ♥ A K 7 3
                    ♦ 8 4
                    ♣ 7
```

This was the bidding:

South	West	North	East
			NB
2♠ *a*	NB *b*	2NT *c*	NB
3♥ *d*	NB	4♠ *e*	NB
NB *f*	NB		

a. South has only 16 high-card points; but with a good chance of making six spade tricks together with the Ace and King of hearts, the hand qualifies for an opening Two-bid. Note that he holds the required four defensive tricks.

b. Tempting to join in, but with a partner who has passed this might prove too expensive. Over an opening bid at the One level it would have been reasonable to make a bid, but now the West hand would have to bid at the Three level, and his suit is simply not good enough.

c. The hand would not be good enough to respond to a One-level opening, but Two Spades is forcing for one round at least, so North gives the negative response of 2NT.

d. Although South is disappointed by partner's negative reply, he has to speak again, and to show the second suit can hardly do any harm.

e. This is the critical bid of the auction. If North simply bid Three Spades the auction would undoubtedly stop dead in its tracks. But look how much better the North hand is than it might have been: it has three trumps in support of partner, it has a doubleton diamond (a possible ruffing value), and it contains an Ace. With any luck these features should be worth two tricks in a spade contract.

f. No reason to be excited – although partner has jumped on the second round, South heard him reply 2NT on the first – denying the material for an immediate positive response, so there cannot possibly be anything better than game available on the hand.

Against Four Spades West led the King of clubs and declarer had to plan the play of the hand with some care. In top winners there were six spades, two hearts and a club; one trick had to be established somewhere. One possibility was the heart suit: declarer and dummy held seven cards in the suit between them and if the missing six cards were divided 3–3, the thirteenth card in hearts could be established as a trick after trumps were drawn. Another chance was that the missing trumps broke 2–2; then, no matter how the hearts divided, the last heart could be trumped on the table after the opponents' trumps had been drawn. But was there any way to get home if the trumps were 3–1 and the hearts 4–2 or worse? It would be no good to draw two rounds of trumps to discover the bad news, for then when the defenders won the third round of hearts they would be able to draw dummy's last trump and South would be left with a second losing heart.

Declarer found an elegant solution. After winning the opening lead with dummy's ♣A, he drew just one round of trumps, then led a low heart from hand! He knew that at least one heart trick had to be lost; how could it cost to give it up now? The defenders now cashed two diamond tricks and played a second round of clubs. Declarer ruffed, drew exactly one more round of trumps to leave one in dummy and one in East's hand, then turned his attention to hearts. If everyone had followed to the Ace and King he would have drawn the last trump and claimed the remaining tricks. But as the cards lay West showed out on the third round of hearts. Now, as a result of South's careful timing, he was able to trump his last losing heart with dummy's remaining trump. East had to follow suit helplessly and declarer was now in a position to make the rest of the tricks with his good trumps.

Declarer's line of play gave him three distinct chances: that the trumps broke 2–2, that the hearts divided 3–3, and finally that the defender with length in hearts also held length in trumps.

It is worth noting that if West had chanced his arm and entered the auction, his side could have found a cheap save. Five Diamonds goes only two off against the Four Spades contract and game that North-South were able to make. A sacrifice of 300 points to save a game would have been worthwhile.

11.

Slam bidding and slam conventions

The real excitement in bridge comes when you and your partner bid a slam – the anticipation as you are waiting for dummy to come down on the table is something that is difficult to describe! However, a question that you may reasonably ask is: what is the incentive to bid and make a slam? The answer is that your side scores a substantial bonus if you succeed in bidding and making a slam. But, note well, you have to both *bid* and *make* your contract of Six or Seven before you gain anything.

For a small slam, which means bidding and making twelve tricks, your side scores a bonus of 500 points if you are not vulnerable (that is, if your side has not yet made a game) and a bonus of 750 points if you are vulnerable.

For a grand slam, bidding and making all thirteen tricks, the bonus is exactly twice as much as for the small slam – 1000 points if your side is not vulnerable, and 1500 points if you are vulnerable. As you can see, that is quite an incentive. But in spite of that, slams are not undertaken lightly. You must always remember that if you advance to Six of a suit and fail to make your contract you are not only failing to get the slam bonus but you are also failing to score for the easy game that your side could have made. And the situation is even more delicate when it comes to bidding a grand slam – if you fail by one trick, not only will the easy game have escaped but you will lose the points that your side could have picked up if you had only bid the small slam.

There are two things that your side needs before it can embark on a successful slam venture – you need the ability to develop twelve or thirteen tricks as the case may be, and you also need a certain measure of control; that is the ability to prevent the opponents taking quick tricks.

Just consider the following two pairs of hands:

a

♠ A K Q J 10 9 8 7	♠ 2
♥ 6 4 2	♥ 7 5 3
♦ K	♦ A Q J 10 9 8 7 6
♣ A	♣ 4

b

♠ A K 3 2	♠ 6 5 4
♥ 6 5 4	♥ A K 3 2
♦ A 3 2	♦ K 5 4
♣ K 5 4	♣ A 3 2

With the hands *a* imagine yourself playing in a diamond contract. You have thousands of tricks in sight (well, to be exact, you have no fewer than seventeen top winners), but there is a nasty hitch – before you start to gather in all of your certain tricks the opponents can cash three top winners in hearts. It is a case of *winners without controls*.

With the hands *b* you have every control in the pack – all four Aces and all four Kings. But your side has not got the values to develop the necessary tricks for a slam contract; indeed, on your unlucky days you might find both the spades and the hearts breaking badly against you and so end with exactly the eight tricks that you started with. This is *controls without winners*.

Clearly these are rather artificial examples, but they illustrate an important principle: that to make a slam you need both winners and controls. Sometimes you will be lucky enough to be dealt a hand on which you only need to find out about a control or two in partner's hand before you can attempt a slam. But far more often it is only the earlier rounds of bidding that give you the clue that your side will be able to develop as many as twelve tricks in the play. An example may help; suppose you had started with:

♠ K 5
♥ K Q J 8 7
♦ A J 10 6
♣ 8 3

Your partner opens One Club and you respond One Heart (you are not quite worth a force of Two Hearts). Over this your partner rebids Four Hearts! Now, think what he is saying: that if you have a bare minimum response of One Heart (perhaps a bare 6 points and a bad four-card heart suit) he thinks that there should be a play for ten tricks in hearts. And you have all these undisclosed values in reserve! There is an excellent case for going on towards a small slam or even a grand slam – your side has certainly got the values, and all that remains is to assure yourself that the opponents cannot take two quick tricks.

Conventions cannot tell you whether you have the values for twelve or thirteen tricks but they can be used successfully to check up on whether your side has enough controls. There are two methods in popular use and you can use both of them (for no extra charge!) depending, of course, on the one for which your hand is best suited.

THE BLACKWOOD CONVENTION

The commonest is the Blackwood convention, named after its American inventor, Easley Blackwood. This convention is used when you want to find out how many Aces partner has got. Note well, how many Aces, not *which* Aces. It is initiated by a bid of 4NT, either by the player who has opened the bidding or his partner. Four No-trumps is a bid that can very conveniently be used as a conventional bid, for who wants to play in a contract of 4NT? Three No-trumps is enough for game, and no more points can be scored unless the partnership is able to bid and make Six or Seven No-trumps. So 4NT can be thought of as an idle bid, and can usefully be harnessed to have an artificial meaning. The player who has to respond to 4NT has no difficult decisions to make; he simply looks at his hand, counts the number of Aces that he holds, and replies as follows:

Five Clubs, if he holds 0 Aces or 4 Aces.
Five Diamonds, if he holds 1 Ace.
Five Hearts, if he holds 2 Aces.
Five Spades, if he holds 3 Aces.

It is a simple enough sequence to remember – the bids are in the same order as the ranking of the suits. Responder makes the cheapest possible reply if he has no Aces, and raises the bidding by one step for each Ace that he holds. There is no real danger of confusion if the reply is Five Clubs; the bidding so far, and whatever the 4NT bidder holds in his own hand will always make it crystal clear whether partner holds no Aces or all four.

Having heard the reply to the question posed by 4NT, the player can, if he wants to, ask partner how many Kings he has got by continuing with a bid of 5NT. His replies are exactly the same as if he were revealing his Aces, except of course they will be one level higher. He will bid:

> Six Clubs, if he holds 0 Kings or 4 Kings.
> Six Diamonds, if he holds 1 King.
> Six Hearts, if he holds 2 Kings.
> Six Spades, if he holds 3 Kings.

If a player goes so far as to ask his partner about Kings, it is clear that he must have been considering the possibility of playing in a grand slam. For the reply to 5NT will automatically commit the partnership to at least Six of whatever suit they are going to play in, no matter how few Kings the responder shows. Logically enough, a player who does bid 5NT must be sure that the partnership hold all four Aces between them, otherwise there would be little point in asking about Kings! Consider an example of Blackwood in action:

West	*East*
♠ Q J 10 9 6	♠ A K 5 4 2
♥ A 5	♥ K Q 7 3
♦ A K Q 10	♦ 9 4
♣ A K	♣ Q 5

Suppose that East opens the bidding with One Spade. After giving West time to recover from his pleasant surprise, let us think of his problem. Spades will certainly be trumps, but such is the power of his hand facing an opening bid that he is not going to be content with just a game. He is interested, purely and simply, in whether the opening bidder has got the Ace and King of spades and the King of hearts. Blackwood is the answer to his problems, and the bidding will go:

West	East
	1♠
4NT	5♦ *a*
5NT *b*	6♥ *c*
7♠ *d*	NB

a. I have one Ace.

b. It must be the Ace of Spades that East holds, as there is only one Ace missing from West's hand. So he asks about Kings.

c. Admitting to two Kings.

d. Now West can count thirteen tricks with spades as trumps.

THE CUE-BID

Although Blackwood is a very useful weapon, it will only solve some of your slam bidding problems. Some of the time it may be far superior to employ the other aid to slam bidding, which is *cue-bidding*. A cue-bid is the bid of a suit in which the player holds a *control* – the Ace, or if the final contract is going to be a suit contract, possibly a void. It has nothing to do with wanting to play with that suit as trumps, so a player must always take care that his partner realises what is the agreed trump suit before he sets out with a cue-bid. Just consider the logic behind this bidding sequence:

West	East
1♠	3♠
4♣	

Now, what can West's bid of Four Clubs mean? He can't possibly be suggesting clubs as an alternative trump suit to spades, for both partners apparently are delighted to play with spades as trumps. Nor can he merely be trying for game in spades, for Four Clubs has committed the partnership to play in at least Four Spades. There can be no misunderstanding here. West's Four Clubs bid carries this message, 'Partner, I am pleased to hear that you like my spades as a trump suit. However, I have a very good hand, and it is possible that we may be able to make Six Spades or even Seven Spades instead of stopping in a game. Unfortunately, just knowing how many Aces you have got will not help me, so I have not used Blackwood. However, I have first round control in clubs (the Ace or a void), and *I would like your opinion on the prospects of a slam.'* That's quite a message to get over in just two words!

How is East expected to react to this sort of bid? It is clear that he cannot just look at his hand and make an immediate reply as he would to Blackwood – he has to use his judgement now! If he is completely minimum for his bid of Three Spades on the first round he will sign off by bidding Four Spades, in an attempt to discourage any further enterprise on his partner's part. However, if he has one of the red Aces and no reason to be ashamed of his original Three Spades bid, he can reply with another cue-bid. If, for example, he held the Ace of hearts his bid would be Four Hearts. There is a vitally important point about this bid. If East had held both red suit Aces, *he would have cue-bid the cheaper one first*. So a bid of Four Hearts, although affirming control in hearts, would specifically deny first round control in diamonds.

To sum up, when a player starts a cue-bidding sequence there are three points to remember:

1. A cue-bid shows first round control in the suit named.

2. It must be obvious that the suit is not being bid with the intention of playing the hand in that denomination.

3. The level at which it is made automatically commits the partnership to game.

Now it is possible for a cue-bid to be made in order to show, not first, but second round control in a suit. There is no danger of this being confused with the first sort of cue-bid that we have already met, for it is only made in a suit where earlier cue-bids have established that the partnership holds first-round control. Consider this sequence:

West	East
1♥	3♥
3♠	4♣
5♣	

After hearts have been agreed as trumps West embarks on a cue-bidding sequence by showing his first round control in spades. East co-operates by showing first round control in clubs, and now West bids Five Clubs. The message here is that he holds second round control in clubs, either the King or possibly a singleton (which will permit him to ruff the second round of the suit). At the same time he is telling East two other things – that he is still not certain enough of his ground to bid Six Hearts, and that he has not got first round control of the other unbid suit, diamonds, for he would have shown this first rather than inform his partner about the second round control. Clearly, the only thing that is worrying West at the moment is the possibility that the defenders will be able to take the first two tricks in diamonds, and he is leaving the final decision as to whether to bid a slam or not to his partner.

Consider one or two hands throughout the bidding, making (we hope) the right decisions as to whether to employ Blackwood or cue-bidding.

Suppose that you had been dealt:

♠ K Q J 10 7
♥ 3
♦ A K Q J 4
♣ 8 2

and heard partner open the bidding with One Spade. You have 16 high card points but that does not give a true picture of your hand's tremendous potential in support of a spade contract by partner. You have five excellent trumps (surely partner has the Ace), a singleton heart, a doubleton club (both possible ruffing values), and a completely solid diamond suit on which partner can take discards. Even if partner has a completely minimum opening bid, you might be able to make twelve tricks, and if he has three Aces, then Seven Spades is not beyond the bounds of possibility. Would you, then, employ Blackwood? Certainly all would be well if he told you that he did hold three Aces: you could go to Seven Spades quite happily. But what if partner held only two Aces? Suddenly you are trapped. It could be, as you don't know *which* two Aces partner holds, that the opposition may be able to take the first two tricks in clubs. This hand should be a dire warning to you: *don't initiate Blackwood unless you are fully prepared for any response that partner may make.*

You see, even with the hand just considered, you may think that if partner tells you he has only two Aces you will be safe enough if you sign off in Five Spades. So you will be, but you may still miss an easy slam if partner happens to hold the King or a singleton in clubs. And missing an easy slam is just as expensive (over the years) as bidding one that offers no play. Suppose these were the two hands:

	West		East
♠	A 9 8 5 2	♠	K Q J 10 7
♥	A K Q J	♥	3
♦	7 3	♦	A K Q J 4
♣	J 6	♣	8 2

The bidding might go:

West		East	
1♠		3♦	*a*
3♥	*b*	3♠	*c*
4♥	*d*	5♦	*e*
5♠	*f*	NB	*g*

a. Creating a forcing to game situation, and promising at least 16 high-card points. Of course, at this point West does not know that his partner has the spades with him.

b. Showing his other biddable suit. Not a cue-bid, as no trump suit has yet been agreed by the partnership.

c. Setting spades as trumps and saying, in effect, that his original force was based on a good fit in spades and a hand too good to bid an immediate Three Spades or Four Spades over One Spade.

d. Now, with spades agreed as trumps, cue-bidding can start. The number of Aces that East has got does not really interest West yet – there are too many gaps in his hand for him to take any decisions. His cue-bid of Four Hearts suggests that he is not minimum for his opening bid, that he has first round control in hearts, and that he has no first round control that he can show more cheaply. With a poor opening bid and no interest in a slam he would have put up the shutters with a bid of Four Spades.

e. Showing first round control in diamonds but denying one in clubs.

f. And I haven't got even second round club control, for if I had I would have gone on to a slam.

g. Reluctantly, but it has become clear that there are two top losers in clubs.

It was a well-bid hand; East-West have no fewer than fourteen winners between them but they were able to diagnose that some vital controls were missing and so put on the brakes in Five Spades.

The important thing about both cue-bidding and Blackwood is that they not only help a partnership to bid slams but, perhaps more important, they allow a partnership to *keep out of silly slams* where there are two top losers.

Now let us try changing the East hand slightly, so that the two hands become:

West	*East*
♠ A 9 8 5 2	♠ K Q J 10 7
♥ A K Q J	♥ 3
♦ 7 3	♦ A K Q J 4 2
♣ J 6	♣ 8

Note the difference; East has gained one more diamond and has lost one of his clubs, so that he now has second round control in the suit. What should East do after an opening One Spade from his partner? It is true that he could still approach his destination by forcing in diamonds, supporting spades and then cue-bidding as he did last time, but now there is a short cut to the same end. He can bid an immediate 4NT (Blackwood) over partner's opening. If partner shows three Aces, East can count all thirteen tricks and there is nothing to hold him back. If West admits to two Aces, East can go on to Six Spades with some confidence, for now he does not mind at all *which* two Aces West holds – whichever one is missing, East can be sure that there is only one loser in that suit. It is just possible that West will have only one Ace, at which discovery East will have to sign off rapidly into Five Spades. But it is scarcely possible that West will have no Aces at all, for then he could hardly hold a genuine opening bid.

NUNES GRAND SLAM FORCE

A third useful weapon for prospective slam bidders is known as the *Nunes Grand Slam Force*. It sometimes happens that when you are investigating grand slam possibilities in a suit, the exact length and strength of the agreed trump suit is uncertain. The player who is about to make a decision as to whether to bid Seven or stop in Six has all the information he needs about controls in the side suits, but perhaps the quality of the trump suit is suspect. If he has not previously used Blackwood (when 5NT would be asking for Kings) he can initiate the Nunes Grand Slam Force by bidding 5NT directly without going through the 4NT routine first. Partner's reply is very simple: with any two of the top three honours in the agreed trump suit, he bids Seven in that suit. With only one of the three top honours he bids Six only.

If you are alert, you may have spotted an obvious objection to this. What happens, you will say, if the responder to the Grand Slam Force doesn't hold the Ace, King or Queen? Well, if there is room for him, he can get over some picture of how many trumps he has at the same time as denying any of the missing honours. Suppose spades are the agreed trump suit and your partner has suddenly leapt to 5NT. You have none of the top honours in spades, but you can show your length as follows:

With only four trumps bid Six Clubs.
With five trumps bid Six Diamonds.
With six trumps bid Six Hearts.

Let us try this out on a couple of hands. Suppose you have been dealt:

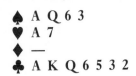

♠ A Q 6 3
♥ A 7
♦ —
♣ A K Q 6 5 3 2

and you are pleased to hear your partner open One Spade. Your sole concern is with the King of spades – although partner is likely to hold it, you cannot be quite sure. And what is more, Blackwood will not help a bit, for suppose partner tells you he has an Ace and two Kings – you still won't know which Kings he has got and ♠K might still be missing. The King of hearts is not nearly so important, for all partner's hearts can be discarded on your clubs after drawing trumps, but the King of spades may represent an inescapable loser. It is vital to find out if partner has got it, and the way to do so is to bid an immediate 5NT over partner's opening. This agrees spades as trumps by inference, and partner's reply will tell all. He can't possibly bid Seven Spades for you have two of the three top honours in spades and there is only one missing. But if he has got the King of spades he will bid Six Spades and you can go happily on to Seven. If the King of spades is missing, he will bid one of the other suits at the Six level and you can return to Six Spades, certain that a vital card is missing and that the grand slam is not worth bidding.

The idea of showing length in the trump suit shows up well on this example:

West	*East*
♠ 6 4	♠ A Q 2
♥ A K J 6 4	♥ 9 8 5 3 2
♦ K Q J 10 3	♦ A 7
♣ A	♣ 9 7 4

As West you open One Heart and partner makes a limit bid of Three Hearts, agreeing hearts as trumps and promising between 10 and 12 points. With 18 honour points and distributional values you decide to investigate slam possibilities and make a cue-bid of Four Clubs. With the Ace of diamonds partner is prepared to go along with the slam idea and responds with a cue-bid of Four Diamonds. At this point, your worry is with the spade suit where you hold no control at all, and you return to Four Hearts. Your reason for failing to continue must be clear, for you have already expressed interest in a slam, so partner is likely to continue with Four Spades to show the Ace. Things have brightened considerably as far as West is concerned: now that partner is known to hold the two missing Aces your only problem is whether to bid Seven Hearts or stop in Six. The critical question is whether or not partner holds the missing Queen of trumps. To find out you bid 5NT. Now partner, who lacks the vital Queen and indeed has no honours at all in the agreed trump suit, has the chance to tell you that he has, however, five-card support. He bids Six Diamonds. Now West is in a strong position. He knows that the Queen of hearts is with the opponents but he knows that his side holds ten cards in the suit and that there are only three missing. It is true that if all three trumps are on your left the grand slam will fail, but if they are divided 2–1 between the opponents or are all on your right (when the missing Queen can be finessed) you will be able to make all thirteen tricks. In fact, this represents nearly 90% chance of success, and the grand slam is well worth bidding.

Finally, an example of cue-bidding in action on a complete deal:

Dealer, South   Love all

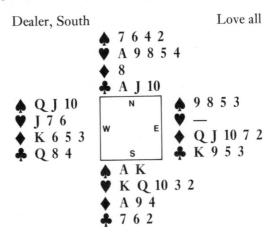

```
                    ♠ 7 6 4 2
                    ♥ A 9 8 5 4
                    ♦ 8
                    ♣ A J 10
♠ Q J 10          ┌─────────┐      ♠ 9 8 5 3
♥ J 7 6           │    N    │      ♥ —
♦ K 6 5 3         │ W     E │      ♦ Q J 10 7 2
♣ Q 8 4           │    S    │      ♣ K 9 5 3
                  └─────────┘
                    ♠ A K
                    ♥ K Q 10 3 2
                    ♦ A 9 4
                    ♣ 7 6 2
```

This was the bidding:

South	West	North	East
1♥	NB	3♥	NB
3♠ *a*	NB	4♣ *b*	NB
4♦ *c*	NB	5♦ *d*	NB
6♥ *e*	NB	NB	NB

a. South is far from minimum, and as Blackwood would not help, starts by cue-bidding his cheapest control.

b. Hearing that partner is interested in a slam, North is pleased to co-operate. He has two Aces, second round control in diamonds, and no reason to be ashamed of his hand.

c. South shows the other Ace; after all if partner has lost interest, he can always sign off with a bid of Four Hearts.

d. Reasoning that as partner is still trying, he might just as well show the second round control in diamonds.

e. Nothing to wait for now.

The play in Six Hearts was not without interest after the lead of the Queen of spades. There were no losers in trumps, dummy's low spades could be ruffed in declarer's hand, and both of South's low diamonds could be trumped on the table. The only problem suit was the clubs, where declarer was missing both the King and Queen. Declarer in fact made the contract by taking two finesses in the club suit – and finessing is a manoeuvre that we won't discuss until we start to talk about the play of the hand as opposed to the bidding. You will have to be patient!

12.

Trumps

A beginner's first reaction when he is told that there is something to be learnt about trumping is often one of incredulity. 'If I haven't got any of a certain suit, I can trump, and there are no problems about that,' is usually his comment. But there is altogether more in the matter than meets the eye: consider first a suit all by itself and forget all about trumps. Suppose that you and your partner hold:

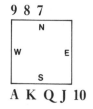

9 8 7

A K Q J 10

You have five certain tricks in this suit. Now make the suit into the trump suit and introduce another suit, thus:

♠ 9 8 7
♥ 4 3 2

♠ A K Q J 10
♥ 5

Suppose the opponents start by leading hearts against your spade contract. You have to follow suit to the first round but you are in a position to trump the second, scoring your first trick from the trump suit. Now there is something curiously satisfying about trumping, particularly if it is one of the opponents' high cards that you are able to ruff. So much so that beginners at the game will go to tremendous lengths to get the lead in dummy (with, perhaps, a diamond or a club) in order to trump again. But after they have done so, and made their second trump trick, what is left? This:

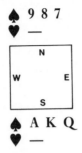

♠ 9 8 7
♥ —

♠ A K Q
♥ —

and with no more possibilities of trumping there are only three tricks to come in the suit. The net result is that declarer has ended with exactly the same number of tricks by trumping as if he had simply led out his trumps.

However, this might have been the starting point:

♠ 9 8 7
♥ 2

♠ A K Q J 10
♥ 5 4 3

Now, if the opponents lead hearts you can trump the second round in dummy, come back to hand with a club or a diamond and trump your last heart. You will have made two trump tricks and still have your own five trumps intact – seven tricks in all instead of five with the trump suit, and you will have *gained* two tricks. It almost looks as though a principle could be stated: that 'trumping in your own hand does not pay, trumping in dummy does' but there are one or two exceptions to this idea. Suppose you had ended up in a diamond contract with J 6 5 4 3 in your hand facing the 2 in dummy. (You may think this impossible. Not so; all sorts of terrible things *can* happen to you at the bridge table.) Now this is a rather different trump suit from the last example – if you set out to *lead* trumps you could easily end with no tricks at all from the suit. Any odd ruffs that you *could* manage to take in your own hand would be something instead of nothing.

A more practical exception would occur if you had started with, say, **A K 10 9** in your hand and found **Q J 8 7 6** on the table. This again is a suit where you have started with five winners. If you had a choice between trumping once in dummy and trumping once in your own hand, the ruff in dummy would give you a trick and leave you with four to come – total five, and no progress. But trumping in hand would still leave you with five more tricks to come.

It is clear now how the principle we tried to formulate should have been stated – *Trumping in the short trump hand gains; trumping in the long trump hand does not.* Indeed, if you trump too many times in the long trump hand you may run out of trumps before you can draw the opponents'.

It becomes clear now why you add on distributional points for shortages when you are supporting your partner's suit – a shortage means that declarer will be in a position to trump in the short trump hand and so make extra tricks. It also becomes clear why an acute shortage like a void is better than a singleton or a doubleton. Look at these three examples, played with spades as trumps:

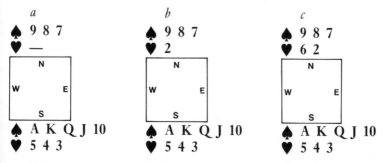

With *a*, given time, you can trump all three losing hearts and so make eight tricks from the trump suit. With *b*, after losing one trick in hearts, you can trump two hearts on the table and collect seven tricks from trumps. And finally with *c*, after losing two tricks in hearts, you will still be able to score one ruff on the table and so collect six tricks in all.

On any hand played in a suit contract there is an ever-present problem – should declarer draw trumps or not? Whist players used to have a saying: 'There is many a man walking the Embankment because he did not draw trumps.' But bridge players often say that there is many a man walking the Embankment because he *did* draw trumps. The truth lies somewhere in between but there are, alas, no hard and fast rules – perhaps the best one that can be concocted is 'draw trumps unless there is a good reason not to'. And, as you can see, that leaves a good deal of scope! Possibly the secret is that a player must learn to recognise the different types of hands, each requiring different treatment. Think of the first of the examples considered above:

♠ 9 8 7
♥ —

♠ A K Q J 10
♥ 5 4 3

With spades as trumps declarer can play to trump all three of his losing hearts on the table, so making three extra tricks from the trump suit. But if he draws all of the opponents' trumps first (and at least three rounds will be necessary as there are five spades outstanding) he will have disposed of all dummy's spades as well, leaving himself with three losing hearts. Even so, drawing trumps could still be the correct play. Suppose that these were the full hands:

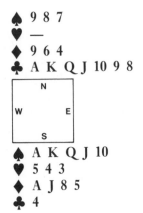

♠ 9 8 7
♥ —
♦ 9 6 4
♣ A K Q J 10 9 8

♠ A K Q J 10
♥ 5 4 3
♦ A J 8 5
♣ 4

and South received the lead of the King of diamonds against his spade contract; there would be *no need* to trump losing hearts in dummy first. Declarer could draw all of the missing spades – playing five rounds if necessary – then run off dummy's club suit to dispose of all his losers. In that way he would enjoy thirteen top tricks with one diamond, five spades, and seven clubs – with absolutely no risk.

The vital test to apply to all hands is 'have you got enough sure winners if you draw all the missing trumps?' If the answer is Yes, then draw trumps. If the answer is No, then ask yourself whether you can use any of the trumps in the *short hand* to give extra tricks.

TACKLING THE PLAY

At this point it will be best to examine a number of typical suit contracts, counting tricks, and making decisions as to how declarer should tackle the play.

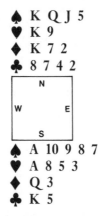

♠ K Q J 5
♥ K 9
♦ K 7 2
♣ 8 7 4 2

♠ A 10 9 8 7
♥ A 8 5 3
♦ Q 3
♣ K 5

South has opened the bidding with One Spade and has been raised to Four Spades by his partner. Against Four Spades West leads the 2 of spades. (Yes, a trump – but that is not all that much of a surprise. Later on, when we discuss opening leads, we will find that a trump lead by the defence is often a paying proposition.) Suppose first of all that South plays another round of trumps and East fails to follow suit. That means that West started with three spades and still has one left. If declarer draws West's last trump at this point, there will be only one trump left in dummy.

Have you seen the trap into which South has fallen? He forgot to count his tricks before he rushed into the play. When dummy came down there were eight top winners in sight – five spade tricks, two hearts, and one winner that could easily be established with the King and Queen of diamonds. It's true that the King of clubs might have proved useful but this was by no means a certainty. Short of tricks for his contract, declarer must ask himself whether he can score any ruffs in the short trump hand. And the answer to that question is yes – there is the chance of trumping hearts in dummy. But after the King and Ace of hearts, South is left with two losing hearts and only one trump in dummy. Clearly three rounds of trumps were too many. Even if South stops after two rounds there is the possibility of West gaining the lead and playing a third round before declarer can ruff his last heart loser – which was why West led trumps in the first place.

Suppose South is allowed another run at the hand (and this doesn't happen at the table!). After winning trump lead in hand the correct line is to play off ♥K and ♥A at once, taking the slight risk that one of them will be ruffed. South then leads a low heart and trumps with dummy's ♠J. There are still two trumps left on the table at this point, and declarer follows with a low diamond towards the Queen in his hand. Say West wins with the Ace and returns another trump – South carefully overtakes ♠Q with the Ace in his own hand (getting the lead where he wants it) and trumps the last losing heart with ♠K. Declarer has made six tricks and has three winning trumps left in his hand together with the now master King of diamonds on the table. With the contract assured there is even a chance of making an overtrick by leading a low club from the table towards the King. If East is the defender who has started with ♣A, South will come to an eleventh trick with ♣K.

Here is another sort of hand where drawing one extra round of trumps might prove fatal:

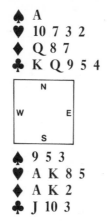

♠ A
♥ 10 7 3 2
♦ Q 8 7
♣ K Q 9 5 4

♠ 9 5 3
♥ A K 8 5
♦ A K 2
♣ J 10 3

Suppose that South is declarer in a contract of Four Hearts after the bidding South – One Heart, North – Four Hearts. The opening lead is the 6 of spades from West. Your first reaction might be that there is no possible objection to drawing all the missing trumps for, even if South makes only two tricks from hearts he will have one spade, three diamonds and four tricks to come from the clubs (once the opposing Ace has been driven out).

But there is also the problem of keeping control of this hand if the trumps do not break well for you. Just imagine what might happen if you started with the Ace and King of hearts and found one opponent had started with four trumps headed by the Queen and Jack. If he was able to get in with the Ace of clubs when you started to play that suit he would be in a position to play off the Queen and Jack drawing *all* your side's trumps. Then the defenders might well be able to take three or four tricks in spades – you would be wide open in the suit and might go several down in your contract of Four Hearts.

It is sensible enough to draw one round of trumps with the Ace, but before releasing the King and with it any measure of control in the suit, you should establish your clubs. You simply lead the suit until the opponents win with their Ace. Then, when you regain the lead, you can play off one more round of trumps and carry on with the clubs. It is true that you might have one of the clubs trumped, but that will be with one of the two possible trump losers. By playing the clubs before clearing trumps you are keeping control of the situation – when in with ♣A the opposition can neither draw trumps (you still have the King) nor cash winning spades (dummy still has three trumps left and no more spades).

Take another example:

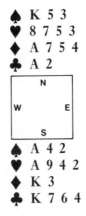

♠ K 5 3
♥ 8 7 5 3
♦ A 7 5 4
♣ A 2

♠ A 4 2
♥ A 9 4 2
♦ K 3
♣ K 7 6 4

Again South plays in Four Hearts, perhaps after the bidding of South – 1NT, North – Two Clubs (Stayman), South – Two Hearts, North – Three Hearts, South – Four Hearts. The opening lead is the Queen of clubs from West. Try looking at this hand from the point of view of losers – tricks that you cannot avoid losing. There is one sure spade loser and (assuming that the missing trumps are divided 3–2) two heart losers. At the moment, however, there are no losers in the minor suits, but if you start the hand by playing off three rounds of trumps you will have manufactured another loser in clubs. Do you see why? Dummy's trumps would normally be able to take care of your two clubs that remain after playing off the Ace and King, but if there is only one trump left in dummy you cannot ruff with it twice! But there is another aspect to the problem on this hand. If you do not touch trumps at all there is the possibility that one of the opponents might over-ruff at some point. And if he was the defender who had started with only two trumps there would still be two natural trump losers to come. What declarer would like to do is draw *two* rounds of trumps exactly – but he may not be able to achieve this if he plays the Ace and another trump, for a defender might be unkind enough to win and play a third round. And that would be distinctly unwelcome.

Actually the solution is quite neat and easy. After winning the club lead declarer should play a low trump *from both hands*, leaving

three trumps outstanding. When South regains the lead he cashes
♥A, leaving just one trump out, and then starts to trump losing
clubs in dummy and diamonds in hand, followed by taking ♠A
and ♠K. At some point the opponent with the winning trump
might be able to over-trump but he will not be in a position to do
any harm – the trick he wins is one that declarer has budgeted to
lose in the first place.

CROSS-RUFFING

There are also hands on which declarer has no interest whatsoever
in drawing trumps. The technical name for play of this nature is
cross-ruffing; declarer's aim in life is to make as many of his trumps
as possible separately, trumping cards both in his own hand and on
the table.

Consider this deal:

```
              ♠ K Q 9 8
              ♥ K J 7 6 4
              ♦ 3
              ♣ K 5 2
          ┌───────────┐
          │     N     │
          │           │
        W │           │ E
          │           │
          │     S     │
          └───────────┘
              ♠ A J 10 7
              ♥ A 3
              ♦ A 9 7 4
              ♣ 8 7 6
```

This time South plays in Four Spades and West leads ♣Q.
Declarer tries the King from dummy but this loses to East's Ace
and a club comes back. West wins the next two tricks with ♣10
and ♣J, then switches to a trump. How should South tackle the
play now? As he has three losing diamonds to dispose of, it would
be disastrous for him to play even one more round of trumps.
Instead declarer should start by cashing ♥A and ♥K, taking the
small but unavoidable risk that one of them will be trumped. Then
he plays off ♦A and, if this stands up, he is home and dry. He
collects the remaining tricks without any danger by trumping

diamonds on the table and hearts in his own hand. Since all of declarer's and dummy's trumps are masters, the defenders cannot over-ruff at any point. Indeed for the last few tricks they will be reduced to under-ruffing helplessly.

A key point to remember, before embarking on a cross-ruff, is that you should *cash any side-suit winners that you have first*. Otherwise you may cross-ruff merrily for a few tricks but then, when you attempt to cash an odd Ace to give you your contract, you receive a nasty jolt when an opponent trumps. He will have seized the opportunity, while you were cross-ruffing, to discard all his cards in this suit! If you had cashed your Ace first, you would not mind what he discarded during the cross-ruff.

Finally, another example hand with points in both the bidding and the planning of the play in the eventual suit contract:

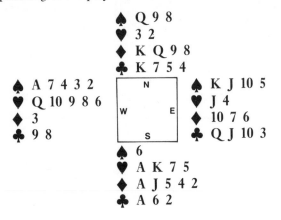

♠ Q 9 8
♥ 3 2
♦ K Q 9 8
♣ K 7 5 4

♠ A 7 4 3 2
♥ Q 10 9 8 6
♦ 3
♣ 9 8

♠ K J 10 5
♥ J 4
♦ 10 7 6
♣ Q J 10 3

♠ 6
♥ A K 7 5
♦ A J 5 4 2
♣ A 6 2

South dealt at game all and this was the bidding:

South	West	North	East
1♦ *a*	NB	3♦ *b*	NB
3♥ *c*	NB	4♦ *d*	NB
5♦ *e*	NB	NB	NB

a South has 17 points and naturally enough bids the longer of the two suits first. However, South's hand is sufficiently strong (and has the right distribution) to reverse into Two Hearts on the next round if the bidding permits.

b North has no major suit to show, but with good four card support for diamonds and 11 points (one added for the doubleton heart) is full value for the limit raise to Three Diamonds.

c Now that diamonds have been supported, South can attach full weight to his singleton spade and is prepared to go on to a game. But it is just possible that North may have an unbiddable four-card heart suit, in which case ten tricks in Four Hearts might be easier than eleven in Five Diamonds. Furthermore, North with guards in both the unbid black suits and little in hearts might be able to bid 3NT. These considerations make the exploratory move of Three Hearts much better than an immediate jump to game in diamonds.

d However, North has not got four hearts, and has not got a sufficiently good guard in spades to hazard no-trumps. So he simply reverts to the agreed suit, diamonds. It is worth noting that, no matter what North's raise to Three Diamonds was based on, he could in no circumstances pass Three Hearts. If he cannot do anything more constructive, as here, he just puts partner back to the suit that they have both agreed will be satisfactory as trumps.

e All the time since hearing partner's Three Diamonds, South has been intending to go on to game. Now that it appears there are no short cuts by way of Four Hearts or 3NT, South advances to Five Diamonds.

Against Five Diamonds West led ♠A. Normally, the lead of an Ace that is not backed by the King is not recommended (see the chapter on Opening Leads), but here West had good grounds for supposing that the other side has little in spades, for they have not considered playing in no-trumps during the bidding. Dummy came down on the table and declarer considered his prospects. Clearly he had done well to avoid 3NT, for the spade situation was distinctly delicate. In Five Diamonds there was a spade loser and another sure loser in clubs. The success of the contract depended on being able to trump both losing hearts on the table. However, South could not afford to have one of his hearts overtrumped by East. There were four trumps outstanding. If they divided evenly the safest play was to draw them, as there would still be two left in dummy to accommodate the losing hearts. After trumping the second round of spades, therefore, declarer played off two rounds of trumps.

There was one precaution that he did take, however, and that was to leave one of dummy's trump honours on the table. Then, if it turned out that West had started with three trumps headed by the 10, it would still be possible to over-ruff him if he was able to ruff a heart ahead of dummy. As the cards lay, declarer was in for a disappointment. Not only were the trumps 3–1, but it was East who still held the missing 10. Denied the easy way to eleven tricks, declarer had to think again. There were two distinct chances. He could trump the third round of hearts with dummy's 9; then if that held he could ruff the last heart high with the King with no danger of an over-ruff. Alternatively, he could draw the last trump and, before trumping a heart, test the clubs. His side had started with seven cards in this suit and there were six missing. If the suit broke 3–3, the thirteenth club would become established as a trick in dummy. It was a question of odds. Correctly, South reasoned that the chance of an even club break was only about 1 in 3, but that the first plan would only fail if, out of the seven hearts that were missing, East held two or less. Clearly this was the best bet, but it simply wasn't declarer's day. He cashed ♥A and ♥K but when he trumped ♥5 on the table the worst happened. East *was* in a position to over-ruff and now there was no way of coming to eleven tricks. It was, at least, some consolation to South to find that the alternative scheme would not have worked either – the club suit was divided 4–2 against him.

Try not to be depressed because South went down in his contract – this does not mean that he and his partner bid badly or played in the wrong contract. Five Diamonds was an excellent resting-place and they would have made eleven tricks perhaps eight or nine times out of ten. That is really all that you can do in the bidding at this game – reach contracts that you will make more often than not. It would be a very dull game indeed if everything always went exactly according to plan. Contract Bridge would never have got off the ground (and it has been played for over forty years) if the game had been completely predictable. And you wouldn't be reading this book!

13.

Finesses

We have already discussed two important ways of *developing* tricks from cards that are not immediate winners. There was the possibility of forcing out whatever high cards the opponents held in order to establish your remaining cards. For example, with:

Q J 10 9

```
        N
  W           E
        S
```

5 4 3

you need only lead the suit twice, losing to the Ace and the King, to give you two tricks with the cards you have left.

There was also the chance of getting low cards to work for you, if your side held enough of them, as in:

A K 8 7 6

```
        N
  W           E
        S
```

5 4 3 2

There are only two top winners, but your side holds nine of the thirteen cards in the suit. That means that the opponents hold only four between them and if the missing cards are divided 2–2 then playing off the Ace and King will drop all the outstanding cards and give you three more tricks to take when you like.

Now is the time to consider another very important way for declarer to come to extra tricks – the *finesse*. Suppose that this is your side's holding in a suit:

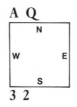

When you start to play the suit you know that there is one vital card missing – the King – and that it is held by one of the opponents. Whether it is East or West who has got it you don't, of course, know at this point. Now, certainly you have one sure trick in the Ace. The problem is to give yourself the best possible chance of scoring a trick with the Queen as well. It will be no use starting the suit from the North hand: if you lead the Ace no one is going to be kind enough to drop the King under it – they will simply wait until the Queen makes an appearance. Equally, you cannot gain by leading the Queen – again whoever has got the King, be it East or West, will just win the trick. But consider the chances if you first lead the suit from the South hand towards the A Q in the North hand. If West, who is the second person to play to this trick, puts up the King your problems are solved – your Ace beats the King and the Queen will supply a second trick. So West, even if he holds the King, will surely follow suit with a low card. Then you have the opportunity to *take a finesse* – you will attempt to win the trick with the Queen from North.

Now is the moment of truth: if West holds the missing King, the Queen will win for East will have nothing with which he can beat it. On the other hand, if the King is with East he will simply take your Queen and the trick. Half the time you win, half the time you lose – that is the essence of a finesse. It is a straight 50% chance of winning an extra trick. Note that well – a chance of an *extra* trick, for if you do not take the finesse or play the suit in any other way you will end up with precisely the one trick that you started with – the Ace.

THE TENACE

A word that you may often hear used is a *tenace*. It describes a holding such as the A Q combination we have been examining. If you will forgive a mildly Irish definition of a tenace, it is a sequence of three cards with the middle one taken away!

Whenever you hold a tenace, you can take a finesse. The principle is the same every time. You must get the lead in the hand opposite the tenace and lead a low card *towards* it. When the hand in between plays low, you play the lower card of the tenace. Then, if the hand that has already followed suit holds the card missing from the middle of the tenace, your play of the lower card stands just as good a chance of winning the trick as the higher card that you are keeping in reserve.

Consider a few finessing positions. In each case we are thinking about a suit in isolation – it does not matter what the suit is, or what contract you are playing in. Your sole aim will be to play the suit in question to the best possible advantage.

Suppose that you had to tackle:

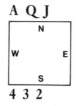

A Q J

4 3 2

This is a suit where, if you liked, you could make two tricks by brute force – cashing the Ace and leading the Queen to force the opponents to take their King and so establishing a second winner for your side with the Jack. But this is also a suit where, if the King is well placed for you, there are *three* tricks available. Clearly you must start with the lead in the South hand. If West follows with a low card, you finesse dummy's Jack. If East turns up with the King, unlucky, but you will not have lost anything – no play could have given you three tricks and at least the Queen has become established as your second trick. But if West is the defender who holds the missing King, you are in the money. The Jack wins the trick and you can *get the lead back to the South hand with another suit* and repeat the winning finesse. This is called a repeated finesse. It is not difficult to visualize a suit in which you have to take a finesse no fewer than three times:

A Q J 10

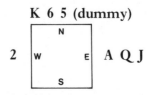

4 3 2

Provided that West holds the missing King and that you can get the lead to the South hand three times, you are in a position to make all four tricks in the suit.

It is worth stressing that the finesses we are discussing are manoeuvres that only *declarer* can try – the situation is rather different for a defender who can see one of his opponent's hands on either his right or his left. Suppose your partner leads the 2 of a suit and this is what you can see from the East seat:

K 6 5 (dummy)

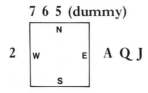

2   A Q J

Declarer plays the five from dummy and it is your turn to produce a card. Naturally enough you win the trick with the Jack and not the Ace. You *know* that the Jack will be good enough. In a sense you are taking a finesse, but it is one that you know will work as you can see the King on your right. But what if partner had led the 2 and this was what you saw:

7 6 5 (dummy)

2   A Q J

Now there would be no temptation whatsoever to try the Jack, as it could not possibly gain. If partner holds the King, any of your cards will do, but if declarer has the King it is essential to play the Ace.

Back to finesses from declarer's viewpoint!

Consider this suit:

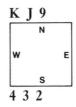

Here declarer might not make any tricks at all if the oppositions' cards are badly placed for him, with East holding **A Q 10**. Then, after leading a low card towards the tenaces in the North hand (**K J** *and* **J 9**), it simply will not matter which card declarer chooses to play as East has just the right card to beat it. On the other hand, if it was West who held **A Q 10** in the suit, declarer would be in comfort – he would lead twice towards the **K J 9** holding and just cover whatever card (short of the Ace) that West played. If he was able to do this twice, there would be two tricks.

This is another common suit holding:

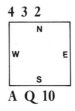

The tenace holdings have been put deliberately in declarer's hand rather than dummy this time to illustrate that it makes no difference. Here there are two important cards missing – the King and the Jack – and of course when declarer starts to play the suit he has no idea where they lie. There are four possibilities (using x to denote an insignificant card):

1.

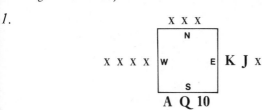

2.

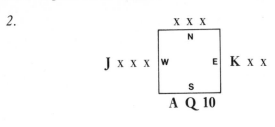

3.

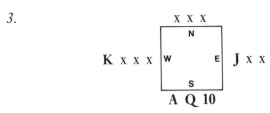

4.

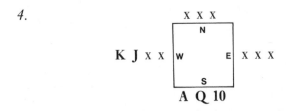

Declarer starts by getting the lead to the North hand and playing a low card in the critical suit. East, of course, follows low (it only removes any guesswork for declarer if he rushes in with a high card) and declarer starts by finessing the 10. If the cards lie as in *1* the 10 wins the trick. South can cross to dummy with another suit and next finesse the Queen. Again this wins and South ends with three tricks. If the cards lie as in *2*, declarer's finesse of the 10 loses to West's Jack. But he does not despair; next time he gains the lead in the North hand he finesses the Queen successfully and comes to two tricks in all. If the cards lie as in *3*, South's finesse of the 10 forces West to win with the King (South's finesse against the Jack has been successful), and with the **A Q** left there is no need to take any more finesses as declarer's high cards are both winners. Only if the set-up is as in *4* is South in for a disappointment. His finesse of the 10 loses to the Jack and later on his attempt to win with the Queen fails as well. He can console himself with the thought that it would not have mattered how he played the cards – there was never more than one trick available. But if he had played the cards differently he would have made fewer tricks in the situations *1, 2* and *3*.

So a player looking at **A Q 10** in one hand and low cards in the other knows that he can make one, two or three tricks in the suit – depending entirely on the whereabouts of the missing cards. At least 75% of the time, the holding will be worth two tricks to him.

A similar set-up would be this:

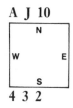

A J 10

4 3 2

Here at least one trick *must* be lost, as the opponents between them hold both the King and Queen and could establish a trick for the defence by force if they were so minded. To give himself the best chance of making two tricks South leads low towards the **A J 10**. If no honour appears on his left (which would solve all his problems) he finesses North's 10. If this loses to the King or Queen, South later attempts a second finesse by leading towards the **A J** and playing the Jack if West follows low. In this way South will make two tricks if West holds at least one of the missing honours and will be restricted to one trick only if East holds both of them. Again there is a 75% chance of making two tricks with this holding.

This, too, is a common suit situation:

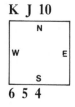

K J 10

6 5 4

To be sure, declarer could come to one trick by force even if he had never heard of finessing. Dummy has three high cards and the defenders have only two cards that will beat any of them. But South has a sensible play for *two* tricks. He leads low from hand, planning to finesse dummy's 10 if West plays low. Then if it is West who holds the missing Queen, the ten will either win the trick or force out the Ace. In either case declarer can return to hand and follow with a finesse of the Jack. If South finds the Queen well-placed (on his left), the **K J 10** combination will be worth two tricks to his side.

Of course you will not always want to take finesses – consider this extreme case:

A K J 10 9 8 7

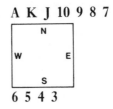

6 5 4 3

Suppose South leads a low card and West follows with the 2. The Queen is missing and it is apparently a straight 50% chance that West holds it. Should then declarer finesse the Jack? Hardly! It would be foolish in the extreme to risk a finesse here, for declarer's side has started with eleven cards in the suit and no matter who holds the Queen it will inevitably fall when the King and Ace are played.

FINESSING WITH AN EIGHT-CARD FIT

However, when you don't hold quite so many cards between the two hands the situation becomes more delicate:

5 4 3 2

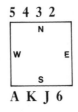

A K J 6

Here you do not want to take an immediate finesse. You should first lead the Ace to cater for the possibility of West holding the singleton Queen. Then, if this chance fails, you cross to the North hand in another suit and finesse the Jack on the return journey, hoping that East will hold the missing Queen. With only eight cards between the hands it is better to play for the 50% chance of the Queen being in a particular hand than for the possibility that the

Queen will fall if you play off the Ace and King.

There are several other suit combinations, where declarer has started with eight cards between the two hands, that are worth examining. Here is another:

Q 10 9 8

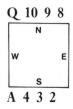

A 4 3 2

One trick must almost certainly be lost, possibly two. But to give himself the best possible chance of coming to three tricks declarer should arrange for the lead to be in dummy. He leads the 8 from the table. Now if East plays the Jack, all South's problems are solved and he is in a position where he can only lose one trick after winning with the Ace. If, however, East covers the 8 with the King, South need lose no tricks in the suit as he wins with the Ace and can now pick up the marked Jack in West's hand. But suppose East follows low: declarer should simply play low from his own hand, letting the 8 run round to West. If the 8 loses to the Jack, declarer re-enters dummy when he next gets the opportunity and leads any one of dummy's remaining cards, again letting it run round to West if East plays low – in effect taking a finesse against the King. As long as East holds one or two honours (the King, the Jack, or both) one trick at most will be lost in the suit.

Another possible combination is:

K J 10 2

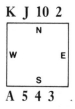

A 5 4 3 .

Declarer should lead the Ace (a safety play) to cater for the possibility of a singleton Queen with East. Then, if this fails, he leads a low card and finesses dummy's 10. Should the 10 win, marking the Queen with West and East shows out, South returns to hand with another suit to repeat the finesse, making all four tricks in the suit.

If, however, East follows suit declarer can be sure that the Queen will follow when he plays off dummy's King. As we decided before, with eight cards in the suit it is better to take a finesse for the missing Queen rather than hope that if falls in two rounds.

FINESSING WITH A NINE-CARD FIT

The situation changes slightly when declarer and his partner have started with *nine* cards between them rather than eight. Clearly the chances of a missing Queen falling are now improved.

7 6 5 4

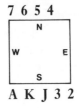

A K J 3 2

With these cards the best play is again to lay down the Ace, and if both opponents follow suit the odds favour continuing with the King rather than taking a finesse. Of course if West shows out on the first round, marking the Queen with East, a second round finesse becomes obligatory.

Take another nine-card fit:

Q 10 9 8 7

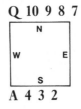

A 4 3 2

Rather than take the double finesse that was the recommended play when your side held only eight cards between the two hands, the best play with this combination is to lay down the Ace. If an honour falls under the Ace you cannot lose more than one trick, but if no honour falls you continue with a lead towards the Queen on the table. Only if East, on your right, has started with K J x or K J x x in the suit will there be two losers.

THE SIMPLE FINESSE

Perhaps the simplest possible finesse position is the following, where there is no sign of a tenace:

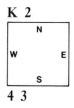

K 2

4 3

Clearly, it will do no good to play the suit from the North hand: leading the 2 will not help as neither opponent is going to help by rushing in with the Ace. They will simply win the trick with something lower and save their Ace to take care of North's King. The only chance of coming to a trick is to lead a low card from the South hand towards North's King. The hope is that West holds the missing Ace. By leading *towards* the King you commit West to playing a card before you choose which one you want to play from the table. If West goes in with the Ace, you play low from the North hand and score your King later. And if West plays a low card, you put up dummy's King and cross your fingers! If West holds the Ace your King will be worth a trick; if East holds the Ace, you will not get anywhere in the suit no matter how you play it. Like all finesses, this is a straight 50% chance.

Very similar is a suit such as the following:

K Q 2

5 4 3

Although you have one certain trick with the King and Queen (you can even lead the King to force out the Ace and establish a trick for the Queen), the best play is to lead from South towards the honours in the North hand. Again you hope that West has got the Ace, for he has to play a card before dummy. If the Ace is well placed for you there are two tricks to be taken by leading twice towards the

K Q 2. And if the worst happens and East turns up with the Ace to kill either your King or your Queen, you will still have the one sure trick with which you started.

The principle behind a lot of these preceding plays, and the last two examples in particular, is that when you have something of value in one hand and nothing in the other, it pays to lead *from* the poor holding *towards* the values in the other hand. Be careful that you do not carry the principle too far – I can always remember a beginner at the game playing this suit:

A K Q J

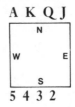

5 4 3 2

Three times he carefully crossed to the South hand before leading a low card towards North's **A K Q J**! Needless to say, the holding of **A K Q J** was sufficiently strong to make four tricks irrespective of which hand led the suit. It is only when there are one or more important cards missing that it pays to lead towards the strength – then, as we have seen, you can get one of the opponents to commit himself to selecting a card before you have to play anything from your strength.

Although it is not quite so easy to identify, the following suit is one of the same type:

Q 3 2

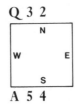

A 5 4

Beginners often tackle a suit like this by leading the Queen from the North hand, hoping to gain if East holds the King and fails to cover the Queen. Alas, this play simply cannot win against sensible defence. If West has the King he beats the Queen with it and all declarer makes is the Ace. If East has the King all he has to do is put it on the Queen. Certainly South makes his Ace, but there will be no more tricks to come from the 5, 4, 3 and 2! However, there is a legitimate chance of making more than the one obvious trick in the suit. South must lead a low card *towards* the Queen. Then if West has the King – your usual 50% chance – you will make a second trick with the Queen, either now or later. Of course, if East turns up with the King you will only make one trick, but that is life.

Remember above all that a finesse gives you a 50% chance of an *extra* trick. Some days it seems that every finesse you take is wrong; other days everything that you try appears to work. But over the years, whether you become an expert or remain a *palooka**, about half your finesses will win and about half will lose.

---

*A *palooka* is the rather unkind name that one bridge player uses to describe another bridge player whom he regards as inferior to himself.

14.   Opening leads and defensive plays

Bridge is not easy for the defenders for two reasons. First, even after the dummy has come into sight, they are not able to see exactly what their side has got in any suit, unlike the declarer who can see all of his side's assets. Second, they have not got nearly so many high cards to play around with as has the declarer – if they had, it would be likely that one of the defenders would be playing the hand as declarer!

One thing is sure, therefore: if you are defending you must try to get good value for such high cards as you hold. It would be unsatisfactory, for example, to win a trick consisting of the 2, 3 and 4 with the Ace if by waiting you might have been able to kill a King or Queen belonging to the other side. However, first things come first, and the first thing that the defenders must do against any contract is to find an opening lead. This is perhaps the most difficult part of defence, for at the time that the opening lead is made the defenders have not yet seen dummy. The player on lead has only the evidence of the bidding and his own hand to guide him.

FINDING AN OPENING LEAD

Ideally, an opening lead should have two properties: it should be constructive, and it should be safe.

By 'constructive' we mean a lead that is doing something useful for the defending side, perhaps establishing tricks, perhaps making it difficult for the declarer to establish tricks.

By 'safe' we mean a lead that does not make a present to declarer of a trick to which he could not have come under his own steam. For example:

```
                    3 2
                 ┌────────┐
                 │   N    │
 A Q 8 7 6       │ W    E │       J 10 9 5
                 │   S    │
                 └────────┘
                    K 4
```

If West *leads* this suit, it does not matter whether he chooses the Ace or a low card. In either case South will be in a position to win a trick with his King. Now if West had refrained from leading this suit and had chosen another one, how could South make a trick with his King? All he can try is to lead low from the North hand towards the King, and when that happens West can put his Ace to full use.

The safest and most reliable opening leads are from a *sequence* of touching cards. No matter how the other cards in the suit are arranged, the lead will not present declarer with anything that does not belong to him. With any sequence the standard lead is the top card, italicised in these examples:

> *A* K Q 4
> *K* Q J 10
> *Q* J 10 9
> *J* 10 9 8
> *10* 9 8 7

You may wonder why the top card is chosen – surely they are all equal in value? Well, of course they are, but your lead is designed to *help your partner* who, you must always remember, cannot see your hand. By sticking rigidly to the rule of leading the top a sequence (and this does not only apply to the *opening* lead but also later in the play), your partner knows where he is immediately. If you lead the Queen, he knows that you have the Jack to back it up but that you have not got the King, and so on.

It must be stressed that we have only been talking about *leading* from a sequence. The situation is rather different when your partner has led a suit in which you have a sequence and you are the third player. Say:

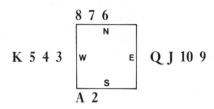

8 7 6

K 5 4 3   Q J 10 9

A 2

West leads the 3 and dummy contributes the 6. Now if you, as East, put on the Queen to lose to South's Ace your partner cannot possibly have a clue as to who has the Jack, 10 or 9. But if you play the lowest card of your sequence, the 9, and this is still enough to force out the declarer's Ace, your partner knows immediately that the missing honours must be in your hand because declarer would not have taken the trick with the Ace if he could have done so with a lower card. This is vital to remember – school yourself to do it without thinking – if you are leading, choose the top card of a sequence, but if you are simply following to a lead, play the lowest of a sequence. So with **A K Q 2** in a suit you would *lead* the Ace, but if the suit is led, you should play the Queen.

Nearly as reliable as genuine sequences of three or more cards are near sequences of this type:

A K J 4
K Q 10 7
Q J 9 3
J 10 8 4

Here you have two touching cards, then a gap, then the next card. From these combinations of cards you make the same lead as if you had a full sequence. The leads are every bit as constructive as sequence leads, but occasionally you will find the opponents' cards arranged in such a way that your lead costs a trick. For example:

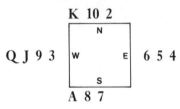

K 10 2

Q J 9 3   6 5 4

A 8 7

If you as West lead the Queen, declarer can win in hand with the Ace and later finesse dummy's 10 to collect three tricks in the suit.

If you had led another suit altogether South would not have been able to come to more than his two obvious tricks. (If South starts the suit by leading low from hand, West puts in the Jack to force dummy's King – then he cannot be prevented from scoring with his Queen.) But look at what went wrong – your lead cost a trick only because your partner held none of the Ace, the King or the 10. Any of those cards would have made the lead safe. Furthermore, the 10 has to be on your left and the top honours divided between North and South. Try it out with South holding the 10, or the Ace and King in the same hand, and you will see that the lead is still safe.

Unfortunately you will not always be dealt suits headed by a convenient sequence. Far more often the suit that you decide to lead may be something like **Q 10 7 5 3**. If you do play a broken suit of this nature, you should lead the *fourth highest* – in this case the 5.

This is a conventional arrangement and something that is universally accepted. If you do anything else you will be, in the words of the old story, the only one in step. You may ask why a lead of the third highest is not best, or even the lowest, but experience has shown that if you always lead fourth highest and *know that your partner does the same* you will gain far more useful information from the opening lead than with any other system of leads. Suppose your partner leads the 2 of a suit against a no-trump contract by the opponents, when he would normally be expected to lead from his longest suit. What can you work out from his lead? Well, if his fourth highest (which he should have led) is his lowest card (and the 2 must be that) you can deduce at once that he has started with only a four card suit. It does not have to be a lead of the 2 from partner to tell you that much.

Consider this case:

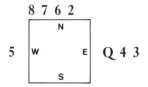

West, your partner, leads the 5 and the North hand appears as dummy. You can see all the cards lower than partner's lead, and can again infer that he has led his lowest card and must have started with a four card suit.

More valuable information comes in when a situation of the following type occurs:

```
              J 10 6
            ┌─────────┐
            │    N    │
      3     │ W     E │   A K 5
            │    S    │
            └─────────┘
```

Your partner, West, leads the 3 and you win with the King. (Remember, the *King* – the lowest card with which you can win the trick.) Sensibly enough, you continue with the Ace. If on the second round West follows with the 2 you know that he started with a five card suit, but if he follows with the 4 you can judge that he had only four cards in the suit originally.

Another useful facet of the fourth highest lead is that you can apply something that is known as the *Rule of Eleven*. This is what the Rule says: *When the fourth highest card of a suit is led, the total number of higher cards in the other three hands is the face value of the card led subtracted from eleven.* It certainly sounds like one of those arithmetic riddles that end up with 'Take away the number you first thought of', but the rule really works.

Take this suit:

```
                 K 5 2
               ┌─────────┐
               │    N    │
  (Q 10 8) 7   │ W     E │   A J 9 3
               │    S    │
               └─────────┘
                  (6 4)
```

After the opening lead of the 7 (fourth highest) by West, the only cards that you, as East, cannot see are those in brackets. Try applying the Rule of Eleven. The face value of the card led is seven; subtract this from eleven to leave four. The Rule says that the North, East and South hands together hold only four cards that can beat West's 7. And from the East seat you can see all four of them – the King in the North hand, and the Ace, Jack and 9 in your own. So South does not hold any cards to beat the 7. At this point a practical application of the Rule comes to light. If declarer plays low from dummy on the lead of the 7, East can follow suit with the 3, secure in the knowledge that partner's 7 will suffice to win the trick. And West, left on lead, can continue the suit to the defenders' advantage.

LEADING AGAINST NO-TRUMPS

So far we have drawn no distinction between leading against a suit contract and leading against no-trumps. In both cases the opening leader wishes to set up tricks for his side and give away as little as possible, but there is a very real difference between the two types of contract.

When you lead the 5 from **Q 10 7 5 3** against no-trumps you hope that your partner will turn up with one or more of the missing high cards. Then you will be able to drive out whatever guards or stoppers declarer holds and establish the remainder of your cards in the suit as tricks. You still choose the same card, the 5, if you elect to lead this suit when there is a trump contract but now your reasons are rather different. Again you hope that partner holds a high card, perhaps the King, when you will be able to establish a trick for your Queen. But it is most unlikely that you will make any further progress in the suit. After you have won with your Queen on the second round somebody, declarer or dummy, will probably have run out of cards in the suit and will be able to trump. It will be of no help to you to have an established suit if the winners are just going to be ruffed.

Against no-trumps you hope to bring in the whole suit; against a trump contract your ambition is limited to one, or perhaps two, tricks with the high cards in the suit.

This does not affect your lead from **Q 10 7 5 3**, but suppose you had started with **A K 7 6 4**. Against no-trumps you still lead your fourth highest, the 6. Then if declarer has only one guard in the suit it will be driven out and whether you or your partner next gain the lead you will be in a position to take four tricks with your remaining cards. To start off with the Ace and King would probably mean that you ended with just two tricks in the suit instead of a possible four. Against a suit contract, however, you only expect to make quick tricks and the Ace is the correct lead. It is most unlikely that your side could ever make more than two tricks in the suit and you have both these tricks ready to take in your own hand. Don't, whatever you do, jeopardize those tricks by leading a low card. If you do so, a likely outcome is that your Ace or King will be trumped by declarer or dummy and a trick will have been thrown away.

Never underlead Aces when something is trumps is an old saying that contains a lot of truth. In other words, if you have a suit headed by the Ace, don't lead a low card against a suit contract. Normally, you would only lead an Ace if it were backed up by the King, so if you were asked the best lead with **A 10 7 3** against a suit contract, the answer would be 'another suit'! As you have seen, however, you need have no qualms about under-leading Aces against no-trumps – they will not run away now and even if the lead appears to give a trick away, it will usually come back with interest.

Against no-trumps it nearly always pays to start off with your long suit. It is extremely rare that you and your partner will have enough tricks in top winners to defeat a sensible contract by the opponents – the only chance of defeating them is to *establish* tricks, and in no-trumps the most promising way of developing tricks is to attack with your long suit in order to get some of your low cards working for you. A possible exception would be if your partner had made a bid during the auction, when you should lead his suit unless your hand presents a very attractive alternative.

Against a suit contract you have a little more choice, as now it often pays to lead a short suit in the hope of securing a ruff before all your trumps are drawn. Singletons are the best bet, but a lead from a doubleton can often work well. If you do decide to lead a doubleton, *always lead the higher of your two cards.*

If you really cannot think of a good, constructive lead on a hand, you can fall back on what is called a 'Top of Nothing' lead. From a holding of **8 7 3**, you would lead the 8. It is not an attractive lead, as you neither have hopes of establishing a trick in the suit, nor of securing a ruff, but occasionally the lead does less harm to your side than any other.

You are now in a position to be able to judge what type of lead your partner has made from the card that he has played. If he has led an honour, you expect it to be the top of a sequence or near sequence. If he has led a relatively low card, then it is his fourth highest in the suit and you can expect him to hold something of value there. Finally, if he has led a fairly high card you can judge it to be the top of a doubleton or possibly top of nothing: in any case you do not expect him to hold any higher cards in the suit.

Unfortunately, singletons come in all shapes and sizes – all you have to guide you in identifying them are the cards you can see in dummy and your own hand, and the bidding.

Try one or two tests. Imagine that in each case your partner, West, has led the 5 of a suit – what do you make of his lead? (In no case has declarer bid the suit in question.)

K J 4 2

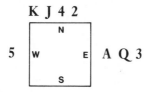

5   W   E   A Q 3

Clearly, this is fourth highest – you can see all the lower cards, so he cannot have led top of nothing. And if the lead were a singleton, declarer would have five cards in the suit and you would have heard something about that in the bidding.

K J 8 7

5   W   E   A Q 6 3

Here you can see that the lead is top of nothing, for five from eleven is six and you can see seven cards higher than the five in both your hand and dummy's. Therefore the lead cannot be fourth highest.

Finally, a more subtle question. What do you make of partner's lead of the 7 here?

K 6 5 4

7   W   E   A Q 8 2

At first sight it could be a singleton, or from 7 3 doubleton, or fourth highest. But think on – if it were fourth highest, what cards would partner have to hold? Yes, you have got it – J 10 9 7. And with a sequence like that he would never have led the 7, but would have chosen the Jack. So you can conclude that partner must have led from a short suit.

It has been suggested that it is good policy to lead partner's suit if he has made a bid. (Certainly it keeps partner happy, which in itself is not a bad thing!) Sometimes this may mean leading from a combination of cards that otherwise you may have left well alone. The following guidelines suggest the best way to give partner a picture of your holding:

> *With any doubleton lead the higher card.*
> *With three cards in partner's suit lead the highest if you have nothing of value, but your lowest if you have an honour.*
> *With four or more cards, lead your fourth highest.*

A few examples would be (with the suggested lead italicised): K 7 *3*, *8* 6 4, Q 8 *7* 3, J 9 *7* 4 2, Q *4*, *9* 5, 10 7 *2* (Yes, the 10 is an honour), *A* 4. There is only one exception to this scheme of leads – if you hold the Ace of partner's suit and there is a trump contract, you don't break the earlier directive about never underleading Aces. The lead should be the Ace regardless of whether you have two, three, four or more cards in the suit.

LEADING TRUMPS AGAINST A SUIT CONTRACT

One final possibility is that of leading trumps against a suit contract. Not, of course, with a view to establishing tricks for your side, but in an attempt to inconvenience declarer. It is difficult to lay down hard and fast rules as to when this is advisable – perhaps the best approach is to consider a few example hands and see how the defender should attack his problem of choosing the best opening lead.

Suppose that, as South, you hold:

♠ K 10 8
♥ 5 4 3 2
♦ K J 10 7
♣ Q 9

and the bidding has gone:

South	West	North	East
			1NT
NB	2♣ *a*	NB	2♥ *b*
NB	4♥	NB	NB
NB			

a. Stayman convention, asking for four card major suits.
b. Showing a four card heart suit.

Well, it is your lead against Four Hearts – which card do you choose, and more important, why? Your reasoning should go like this: the opponents think that they can make more tricks with hearts as trumps than in no-trumps. In defence you are most unlikely to make a trick with your trump holding, but you can put your trumps to good use by leading them. If, as sounds likely, the opponents have found a 4–4 fit, it means that every time you lead a trump you will be using up two of theirs – one from dummy and one from declarer's hand. As they wanted to play in hearts, presumably dummy will have some ruffing values, but what good will they be to him if he hasn't got any trumps left? Another independent reason for choosing a trump lead is that it is less likely to cost your side a trick than anything else. To lead from one of the other suits could well present declarer with a trick that he could not have made if left to his own devices.

Bridge is a game that seems packed with old sayings, some giving good advice, some not so good. Under the latter heading comes 'When in doubt, lead trumps.' However, there is some backing of sense in the idea. Suppose you were on lead against a heart contract with:

♠ K 10 7 3
♥ 9 8
♦ A 9 5 2
♣ A Q 6

On the previous example there were several positive reasons for leading trumps, but with this hand the trump lead is recommended purely for the reason that it is the lead least likely to give away a trick. It is really a case of leading trumps because it is the least unattractive lead!

There are many times when the bidding suggests a trump lead. One situation where this is true occurs when your partner has doubled the opponents (for penalties) at a *low level*. This can only be based on good trumps – how else could he be confident enough to double at a low level? And your trump lead could well help your partner to draw all of the enemy's trumps early in the play. Another situation is one in which you feel that you and your partner have more high card strength than the opponents who, nevertheless, have bought the contract. They can only be relying on ruffing values to give them tricks, and the more rounds of trumps that the defence can fit in, the better it will be for them. So often a well-judged trump lead may be the only way to defeat a close contract.

Unfortunately, no one rings a bell to warn you that you should be leading trumps. You have to consider every case on its individual merits. Try this one. As South you hold:

♠ 10 7 2
♥ Q 8 5 4
♦ A 6
♣ Q J 3 2

and the bidding has gone:

South	West	North	East
			1♠
NB	2♠	3♦	Dble
NB	3♠	NB	NB
NB			

Your immediate impulse is to lead the Ace of partner's suit, but here the bidding has been very helpful. Your partner has joined in at the three level and must have at least a five-card diamond suit and probably a six-card suit. East has doubled (for penalties, of course, since his partner has made a bid) and can be expected to hold at least four cards in the suit. You have two, so West is likely to hold only a singleton diamond, or possibly none at all since he did not fancy the prospects of defending against Three Diamonds doubled and removed to Three Spades. Given a free run, declarer may be able to trump most of his diamonds in dummy. You do not want to help him on his way by leading diamonds – a far more effective attack would be a trump to reduce dummy's ruffing power.

One final example – as South you hold:

♠ 4
♥ J 10 9
♦ Q 10 7 3
♣ K 9 7 4 2

and the bidding has gone:

South	West	North	East
			1♠
NB	1NT	NB	2♥
NB	4♥	NB	NB
NB			

The bidding is highly significant. On the first round West makes a limit bid of 1NT (suggesting 6–9 points). But when East says that he does not like the idea of no-trumps and removes to Two Hearts, it appears that the West hand improves considerably with a very good fit in hearts. So much so that he jumps to game in hearts in spite of the fact that East might have a completely minimum opening bid. It seems fairly sure that West is short in spades and hopes to ruff, and equally sure that your partner has length in spades as you have only a singleton. Rather than try to develop tricks in either of your minor suits, a trump lead stands out a mile. You must make an *immediate* start on cutting down the improved value of West's hand.

GETTING THE BEST VALUE FROM YOUR HIGH CARDS

So much for opening leads – not an easy topic as was suggested at the beginning. Later on in the play the defenders' problems will not be so acute; at least they will have had a chance to study dummy. However, they still have to take care that they get the best possible value for whatever high cards they hold. Perhaps this point is best illustrated with a simple example:

K 4 2

A 7 6   W   E   J 10 9 8

Q 5 3

Suppose South, the declarer, leads a low card from his hand. West can win this trick with the Ace if he wants to, but is this best for the defence in the long run? Rushing in with the Ace collects the 2 and the 3 from the opposition and the declarer will have no trouble in making two tricks later on, one with the King and one with the Queen. Now if West had played low on the first trick it is true that dummy's King would have been able to win the trick, but that would have been the last trick that declarer came to in the suit. West simply saves his Ace until the Queen makes an appearance.

Alternatively, South may start the suit by leading the Queen. If West puts his Ace on, he gets good value and declarer will be held to one trick only with dummy's King. But if West had allowed the Queen to win he would have been powerless to prevent South scoring a second trick in the suit by leading a low card towards the King on the table.

To help the defender in this sort of situation we can again fall back on two adages, dating back a century or more to whist playing days. They are: *Second hand plays low* but that he should *Cover an honour with an honour*.

You may wonder why the emphasis is placed upon the second player to a trick. Well, we have already considered the worries of a player who leads – the first player. The third player does not have a great deal to concern him for it is his partner who has led the suit. In principle, he will do the best he can to help his partner. The last player to any trick has the easiest job of the lot: he can sit back and look at the three cards on the table. If the trick already belongs to his partner there is nothing to be done. If the trick is being won by the opponents he will win if he can, and will win as cheaply as possible. This is why it is absolutely delightful to be the fourth player to a trick if you hold something like **A Q 10** in the suit. Whatever is played you can win the trick economically. If you could only be last to play for two rounds of this suit you would be assured of three tricks, but if you had to *lead* the suit you might end up with only one trick.

Certainly the two old sayings work out for the best in the example above, but they could be carried too far. No one is recommending that with **A K Q J 2** you should follow with the 2 if a low card is led on your right – you will have a lot of explaining to do to your partner if declarer scores a trick with the 10! Nor is anyone suggesting that if a King is led on your right you should gravely cover it with the Queen – strictly speaking the saying should run *Cover an honour with a higher honour if you can*. But even then the rule has exceptions as will become clear in the examples that follow.

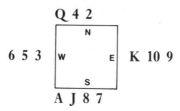

If North leads the Queen, East should cover with the King. In that way he will win the third round of the suit with his 10. But if he plays low on the lead of the Queen, declarer will make tricks separately with all of his honours and East's King will fall helplessly under the Ace without having achieved anything in life.

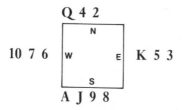

Again, if the Queen is led East should cover. The effect will be to *promote* his partner's 10 and West will be in a position to win the third trick in the suit. If East fails to cover, the Queen will win the first trick, a finesse of the Jack the second, and East's King and West's 10 will both tumble down beneath South's Ace – with just as much effect as if they had been the 2 and the 3.

However, there are situations in which it does not pay to cover an honour with an honour. Try this one:

Q J 10 9

8 7   W   E K 4 3 2

A 6 5

If East covers the lead of the Queen with the King, declarer makes all four tricks in the suit. It is true that if East plays low, so will South, and dummy's Queen will win. But East can withhold his King until the fourth round of the suit and South has to play his Ace on the third round (he has only three cards in the suit); so at least East can restrict declarer to three natural winners instead of four.

Generally speaking it pays to cover when single honours are led, but not when the honour that is led is one of a sequence. Unhappily, even that suggestion has some exceptions in practice – you were warned that defence was not easy!

Sometimes a defender can spot an independent way of solving his problem of whether to cover or not. Take this situation:

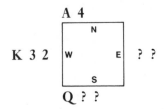

Suppose South leads the Queen from his own hand. Should West cover? Not being able to see the rest of South's cards he does not know whether the Queen is backed up by the Jack or not. But West can save his King until the third round without any worries as he knows that dummy's Ace must be played on one of the first two tricks.

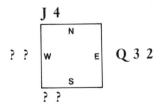

Suppose that this is the spade suit and that South has opened the bidding with Four Spades after which everyone has passed. Declarer wins the opening lead in dummy and plays ♠J. Should East cover or not? The answer comes easily if you remember *why* you cover an honour with an honour. It is in the hope of making declarer use two high cards on one trick, thus promoting an intermediate card for either you or your partner. Well, your 3 and 2 can never be promoted to trick-taking status, and how many cards can your partner hold in this suit? South's pre-emptive opening marks him with at least a seven-card suit. You have three spades, and dummy two. That means at most a singleton for your partner, and in that case he cannot possibly have anything that can be promoted – his only card is going to appear on the present trick.

This could have been the complete suit:

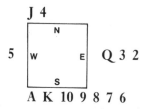

Declarer led the Jack to see if he could tempt you into covering, when all his problems in the suit would be solved – remember he does not know that you hold the Queen. If you play low without thinking too long about the matter, South may well put on his Ace and play for the drop of the Queen – sensible enough with nine cards between the two hands and only four missing. There is a hidden trap here – if, on the lead of the Jack you study the ceiling for some while and eventually play low it will not need Sherlock Holmes to deduce that you were wondering whether or not to cover. Declarer will place you with the Queen and take a successful finesse.

In case you think that it might be a good idea to try to deceive the declarer by thinking for some while when you only have the 3 and the 2, the answer is *NO*, it would not. You might succeed the first time that you try it, but you just wouldn't be invited to play there again! To think when you have absolutely nothing to think about is regarded as actively unethical – almost akin to cheating, or at the very least sharp practice.

It may sound terribly difficult, but the perfect defender plays all his cards at exactly the same speed – in that way, whether he is in difficulties or not, he will not let declarer know about it!

15.   The hold up

It sounds like the title of a Western, doesn't it? But bridge players have a lot of colourful names for their plays and conventions (and occasionally for their partners too!) and this one, as you will see, is very descriptive.

From the way we have been talking about the proper use of high cards in the last chapter you may have got the impression that if you see a King that belongs to an opponent you could not possibly do better with your Ace than to win this trick. Well, there are circumstances in which it may pay you to keep your high card back for the time being – to *hold up*.

Take this hand:

♠ Q J 5
♥ A 7
♦ A 8 5 4
♣ K J 10 2

♠ A K 3
♥ 8 5 2
♦ K 7 2
♣ A 6 5 3

This was the bidding:

South	West	North	East
1NT	2♥	3NT	NB
NB	NB		

and against your contract of 3NT West leads the King of hearts. Don't rush at the play – it always pays to study dummy, count your tricks, and form some plan of campaign before playing to the first trick.

Your first reflection should be that your side holds 29 points, leaving only 11 for the opponents. Now West has made a bid, presumably based on a long heart suit as it was an overcall at the Two level, and it seems likely that he must have most, if not all, of the missing points. Having got that far, the next task is to count how many tricks you can make without losing the lead. You have three spades, one heart, two diamonds and two clubs 'on top' – that makes eight sure winners. But you are in 3NT and require nine tricks in all. It is clear that the ninth trick must come from clubs, either by taking a finesse or by finding the missing Queen singleton or doubleton. Of course, the problem is that if you lose a trick in clubs early on the opponents can take enough tricks in hearts to set the contract. With one solitary guard in hearts there is no rush to take your trick and the correct play is to hold off. Undoubtedly West will continue hearts and this time you are forced to win with your Ace. At this point West will have established the rest of his heart suit as winners and will be able to enjoy them – *if he ever gets the lead.* Now if West had started with a six-card heart suit his partner will have held only two originally, and as a result of your hold up play he will no longer have any cards in the suit. So if you now take a club finesse into East's hand (after playing the Ace first, in case the Queen is singleton) you won't mind if it loses to East's Queen. Your ninth trick will have been established and East can do you no harm with his return. Of course, it may have been West who held ♣Q all the time but in that case the club finesse will win and you will have your ninth trick anyhow.

Even if there had been no opposition bidding against you, it would cost nothing to hold up ♥A until you are forced to take it. By playing the clubs in the same way you will make your contract every time that West has started with a six-card heart suit. And if it turns out that the hearts broke 4–4, then any play would have won (you can lose at most three hearts and one club), but you will have lost nothing by holding up. Just like taking a finesse, if a play cannot lose and may gain it is a play worth making.

Now try another example of a hold up play which is considerably more subtle than the one above. Suppose these are the North-South hands:

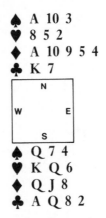

♠ A 10 3
♥ 8 5 2
♦ A 10 9 5 4
♣ K 7

♠ Q 7 4
♥ K Q 6
♦ Q J 8
♣ A Q 8 2

As South you open One Club (although you have the right distribution, you have the wrong number of points to open 1NT) and West overcalls with One Heart. North bids Two Diamonds and when this comes round to you it is sensible, with 16 points and a good guard in the opponents' hearts, to bid 2NT. North raises to 3NT, for your bid of 2NT has suggested that you have the same sort of hand that would have rebid 1NT over a response of One Diamond had there been no interference bidding – in other words 15 or 16 points. So North, with his 11 points, can judge that there will be a reasonable play for game.

Against your contract of 3NT West leads ♥J and now it is up to you to acquire nine tricks. Remember the drill: take your time, study the dummy and decide how many top winners you have before playing to the first trick. At first sight there is one heart trick (on the lead), one spade trick, three club tricks and a diamond trick. Only six tricks 'on top', but the diamond suit is very promising. Apart from the Ace, if the King of diamonds is right the suit will give four extra tricks, and even if ♦K is badly placed, three extra tricks – apparently ample for your contract. But the extra tricks in diamonds can only be brought into play after taking a finesse into East's hand; and this may have been the full lay-out:

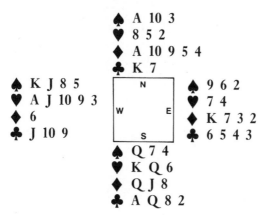

Can you see what happens if you win the first heart trick and finesse in diamonds? East wins with his King and returns a heart. Then, whatever you play from hand, West will have four heart tricks to take which, together with ♦K, will spell defeat for your contract of 3NT.

Although there are circumstances in which it might mean giving up a trick unnecessarily, South should allow the opening lead of ♥J to win. What can West do? Suppose that he continues with Ace and another heart to establish the rest of the suit. Now declarer can take the diamond finesse into East's hand, secure in the knowledge that, even if it loses, East will have no more hearts to play.

USING THE HOLD UP IN DEFENCE

The defenders as well as declarer can use the hold up to their advantage. Take the following example hand:

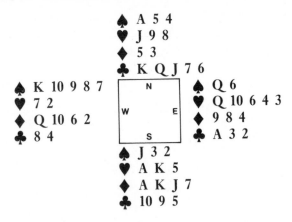

```
                    ♠ A 5 4
                    ♥ J 9 8
                    ♦ 5 3
                    ♣ K Q J 7 6
  ♠ K 10 9 8 7                      ♠ Q 6
  ♥ 7 2                             ♥ Q 10 6 4 3
  ♦ Q 10 6 2                        ♦ 9 8 4
  ♣ 8 4                             ♣ A 3 2
                    ♠ J 3 2
                    ♥ A K 5
                    ♦ A K J 7
                    ♣ 10 9 5
```

The bidding was short and to the point: South (too strong to open
1NT although he held the right distribution) started with One
Diamond and North responded Two Clubs. With a better than
minimum opening bid South was able to rebid 2NT, suggesting
15–16 points, and North was happy to raise to game in no-trumps.

Against 3NT West chose to lease ♠10. It is worth noting this
lead, as West did not play the orthodox ♠8 which would have been
his fourth highest. In fact he led what is termed the 'top of an
interior sequence' – quite a common choice from suits such as
Q *10* 9 8 7, K *J* 10 9 8 or A *J* 10 9 8 against no-trump contracts. In
each case the italicised card is the top of an interior sequence.

From declarer's point of view the defence had struck the most
worrying lead. It attacked dummy's entry (the Ace of spades) to the
clubs before the suit had been established. Before starting to play
declarer counted his top winners. Things were not very promising
with one spade, two hearts, and two diamonds as the only tricks
immediately available. However, dummy's club suit offered
prospects for the four extra tricks that were required. The immediate problem was the spade suit which the opponents had attacked.
There was the outside chance that West had led away from both
the King and Queen of spades, but in any case there was no rush
to win with ♠A, so declarer played low from the table. East won
with the Queen. It was clear that his partner had found a good lead
from K 10 9 8 (the lead marked declarer with ♠J; remember that
the lead of an honour always denies the one immediately above
and with K J x in the suit he would surely have taken the first trick.

East then returned ♠6. It would have been foolish to try a heart at this point, for if one defender leads one suit and the other defender attacks another, the likely outcome is that neither suit becomes established. Furthermore, East was keen on driving out dummy's ♠A – the only outside entry to the long club suit.

South tried the Jack of spades from his own hand but West covered with the King. Again declarer ducked, hoping against hope that the defenders would switch to some other suit. No such luck, however, for West played a third round of spades and dummy was forced to win. Now declarer started on clubs, hoping that it was not West, who was known to hold two winning spades, who got in with the Ace, for then he would have enough tricks to beat the contract out of hand. But it was East who held ♣A, and with no great incentive to take the lead it was his turn to employ the hold up: he kept back his Ace of clubs until the third round of the suit. Declarer was allowed to make two tricks in clubs, and had two more ready established on the table, but there was no way to get the lead there to enjoy them.

As a last resort South played off the Ace and King of hearts, hoping that the Queen would fall in two rounds, when ♥J would afford an entry to the table. However, the Queen did not appear and when the Ace and King of diamonds failed to bring any joy, South had to be content with seven tricks, going two off in his contract of 3NT.

This does not mean that 3NT was an over optimistic contract or that South played badly – all sorts of things might have happened that would have enabled him to get home. West might not have had a natural spade lead, and without the spade attack there would have been no problems. Furthermore, East might have started with ♣A alone, or possibly ♣A x, in which case he would not have been in a position to hold up his Ace until the third round of the suit. Finally, you must remember that East-West found a perfect defence: Nine times out of ten it doesn't go like that – someone does something silly to help you!

16.   Defensive signals

In earlier chapters we have discussed why defending is such a difficult affair, the defenders never being in a position to judge just what their side holds in a particular suit. Some players never seem to make the effort to defend well – they feel that if declarer made enough tricks for his contract there was little that they could do about it, while if declarer went off it was their good fortune rather than good stage management. And yet defence is a vitally important part of the game. Only half the time will your side be playing the hand and on half of those occasions you will be the dummy, taking no active part in proceedings. *You will be defending twice as many hands as you will be playing as declarer.*

A vitally important way for the defenders to help one another is by *signalling*. Let us get one thing straight immediately – signalling is not nodding and smiling if you like your partner's lead, or the sharp exhalation of breath and accompanying scowl that has been known to greet a play of partner that fails to meet with your approval. Such activities have absolutely no part in the game of bridge. Do not get the idea that the game can only be played in an atmosphere of gloomy silence – far from it, but you must lean over backwards in your efforts to give partner no clues at all from your demeanour as to what you might want him to do. Only if the game is played in that spirit can it be completely enjoyable.

Fortunately there are legitimate ways in which the defenders can exchange information. They can convey messages to each other by the cards that they play when they follow suit, and the cards that they discard. Take a simple instance:

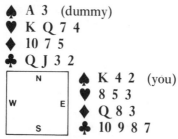

♠ A 3 (dummy)
♥ K Q 7 4
♦ 10 7 5
♣ Q J 3 2

♠ K 4 2 (you)
♥ 8 5 3
♦ Q 8 3
♣ 10 9 8 7

The opponents have reached a contract of Four Hearts and your partner leads the Ace of diamonds, dummy following with the 5. Now your partner's lead suggests that he has the King to back up his Ace (remember, it is not good defence to blaze away with Aces unless they are supported by Kings). You have the Queen of diamonds and it is possible that the defence will be able to take the first three tricks in the suit. You want your partner to continue leading diamonds by cashing the King and leading another one to your Queen.

THE PETER

You convey the message by following suit with the 8 of diamonds – an unnecessarily high card, which your partner will take as a signal to continue leading the suit. And you will confirm the message on the second round, when he leads ♦ K, by following with the 3. This 'high-low' play is known as a *peter*, or sometimes an *echo*, and is encouraging. Often partner can tell from the size of the first card that you play that you are beginning a peter, but sometimes he will have to wait until he has seen your second card before he can be sure. You might have started with Q 3 2 in the suit when your first play of the 3 will not look at all encouraging. However, when you produce the 2 on the next round partner will realise that you have petered. (A word of warning! If you have not been in the habit of sorting your low cards too accurately, now is the time to start. There is a world of difference between following suit with the 2 then the 3, and the 3 then the 2.)

There is a natural corollary to the above. If you want to *discourage* your partner from continuing his suit, or can see no good reason for wanting him to carry on, you should play your *lowest* card. If, in the example above, you had started with ♦ 8 3 2, the correct play would be to follow to partner's Ace with the 2. Incidentally, you can see just how useful the Two's in your hand can be – they are cards that you can be sure your partner will interpret as a sign of discouragement.

It pays to make your signals as clear as possible. If you held **A 8 3 2** in a suit and partner led the King, you want him to carry on. Don't put on the 3 and hope that he notices the 2 is missing – signal with the highest card that you can afford – in this case the 8.

There are other situations in which you want partner to continue leading his suit. Still defending against Four Hearts, let us change the example slightly:

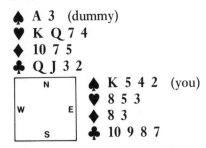

♠ A 3   (dummy)
♥ K Q 7 4
♦ 10 7 5
♣ Q J 3 2

♠ K 5 4 2   (you)
♥ 8 5 3
♦ 8 3
♣ 10 9 8 7

Again partner leads the Ace of diamonds. Although you don't hold the Queen, you still want him to cash the King and lead a third round which you will be able to trump – a trump trick that otherwise you would have had no chance of making. So on the first round you encourage with the 8 and on the second round you complete your peter by dropping the 3.

You do not have to wait until your partner cashes an Ace before you can signal encouragement or otherwise. Take a suit like this:

A 7 6   (dummy)

3   K 9 2   (you)

Your partner leads the 3 of the suit and declarer wins with the Ace in dummy. As you are not required to try to win this trick, you have a free choice as to which card you play. You should drop the 9 under dummy's Ace with the message that you are pleased with your partner's choice of lead and hope that he will continue with the suit on the next occasion that he gets the lead.

There is one trap to look out for:

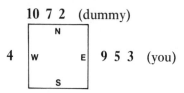

10 7 2 (dummy)

4   9 5 3 (you)

If your partner leads the 4 and declarer plays the 2 from dummy, it is tempting to contribute the 3 in an attempt to warn partner that you do not approve of his lead. Tempting, but very wrong! In the examples considered so far, either your partner or dummy has already won the trick – you were not called upon to make any effort in that direction. But in this situation, you simply have to do the best you can to win the trick. The 9 is a poor best, but there it is. If the remainder of the suit was distributed in this way:

Q J 6 4   (partner)

A K 8   (declarer)

failure to play the 9 would result in declarer getting a cheap extra trick with his 8, and he would still have the Ace and King to come later.

SIGNALLING THE NUMBER OF CARDS IN A SUIT

Another important role signalling can play in the defence is to tell your partner how many cards you hold in a suit. Take this situation:

K Q 10 8 3   (dummy)

A 7 5   (partner)   9 2   (you)

J 6 4   (declarer)

Suppose that South is playing in a no-trumps contract and that dummy has no obvious entry in any other suit. Declarer leads the

Jack from hand and, quite rightly, your partner holds up his Ace. Now, if you were to play the 9 on this trick, is there any possible danger that partner will think that you are trying to encourage him to play this suit? Hardly, for like you partner can see the length and strength of the suit in dummy. A peter in this situation carries quite a different message from the one we considered before. It announces that *the player who peters has started with an even number of cards in the suit.* In this case there will be no doubt in West's mind that it is a doubleton that you are showing. And if he knows that you have got two cards in the suit, he knows that declarer has started with three cards and that to shut out dummy's suit it will be necessary to hold up his Ace until the third round. On the other hand, if you had started life with **9 4 2** (leaving **J 6** for declarer) you follow suit on the first round with the 2. Partner knows that you have not begun a peter, and so must have started with an *odd* number of cards in the suit. It is not difficult for him to gauge that this must be three (if you have a singleton he will not be able to hold up his Ace enough times to shut out the suit, for declarer will have four cards), and he can put his Ace on the *second* round of the suit. In that way dummy's winners are shut out just as effectively as if he had saved his Ace until the third trick but with the added advantage that declarer has been allowed to win only one trick in the suit.

See how the idea works out in practical play; imagine that you are sitting South and are declarer in 3NT.

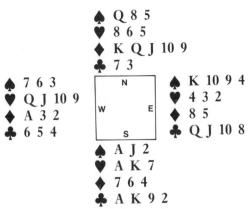

The choice of opening lead sets West no problems; his longest suit is headed by a sequence so the Queen of hearts is a natural selection. Dummy appears and you take stock. You have only five tricks in top winners, but with the Queen and Jack of spades there will be another trick to come from that suit. To get to the nine tricks needed for 3NT the diamonds will have to supply the extra three tricks. There will be no problem if the Ace of diamonds is singleton or doubleton in either defender's hand as they will not be able to hold the Ace up enough times to inconvenience you. Furthermore, if West holds the King of spades, it will be possible to use ♠Q as an entry to the table. The immediate problem is the heart lead – it cannot cost anything to hold off and it may be possible to cut the defender's communications.

After you have played low to the opening lead from dummy, East has the opportunity to make a signal – by following suit with the 2 he suggests that he has nothing of any great interest in the suit. However, when the Queen of hearts is allowed to win West can see nothing better but to continue the hearts and this time you are forced to win with the King.

Clearly you must make a start on the diamonds: you lead low from hand and West is not hard pushed to hold off. The nine from dummy wins the trick and now East makes his second signal – he drops ♦8, petering to show an even number of cards in the suit. At this stage West knows that you have started with three cards in the diamond suit and nothing is going to persuade him to use his Ace when you follow with ♦10 from dummy. In fact on the next diamond lead East completes his peter by following with the 5 and, as expected, West holds up again. This, of course, is bad news to you as declarer. It means that the Ace of diamonds was neither singleton or doubleton. Just think, if you had been playing against less careful opponents who did not watch the cards that their partners played, you might have been home and dry by now!

The only hope left is to dislodge the Ace of diamonds and hope that ♠Q will provide an entry to dummy and that the defenders will not be able to take more than one extra trick in hearts. Accordingly you lead a third round of diamonds to West's Ace and, although he has no hope of getting in to make his thirteenth card in the suit, he gets off play safely enough with a heart to your Ace.

At least the heart suit was divided 4–3, and you still have some hopes, for if West holds ♠K there will be only two more tricks to lose. First you lay down ♠A, just in case someone had started with the singleton King. However, nothing falls and when you continue with a spade to the Queen, to your disgust it is East who turns up with the King. Now there is no hope left – East returns a spade and you score with ♠J, but at the end you have to surrender two club tricks for one down. The key to the successful defence was West holding up ♦A until the third round, having followed his partner's signals closely.

THE LEAD DIRECTING SIGNAL

This signal can be used when you have a good holding in a suit and want to let partner know about it so that he can play the suit when he gains the lead. If you get the chance you discard an un-necessarily *high* card from the suit at the first opportunity – not a *low* card, which would suggest that you did not want the suit led. Suppose that as East you are sitting over dummy in this situation:

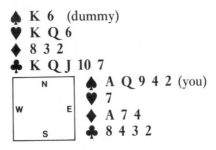

```
          ♠ K 6   (dummy)
          ♥ K Q 6
          ♦ 8 3 2
          ♣ K Q J 10 7
     ┌─────────┐  ♠ A Q 9 4 2  (you)
     │    N    │  ♥ 7
     │ W     E │  ♦ A 7 4
     │    S    │  ♣ 8 4 3 2
     └─────────┘
```

The contract is Four Hearts and your partner leads ♦6. You win with the Ace and return ♦7 but to your disappointment declarer wins with the King. South now sets to work on trumps, leading low to dummy's King and continuing with the Queen. You have to discard and here is the opportunity to let partner know about your holding in spades. When he next gets in you want him to lead a spade through dummy's K 6 so that you will be able to score two tricks with your A Q tenace. Your first discard should be ♠9. Without this lead directing signal, your partner might have con-tinued diamonds when he got in and your chance of making two spade tricks might disappear out of the window as declarer might be able to throw all his losing spades away on dummy's club suit.

THE MCKENNEY SUIT PREFERENCE SIGNAL

Like the Stayman convention, this is named after its inventor. This is how it works: when you lead a suit that you are confident your partner will ruff, you can at the same time suggest which of the *other* two suits (excluding the one you are leading and the trump suit) you would prefer him to play back after taking his ruff. If you lead a *high* card for him to trump you want the *higher-ranking* of the two other suits led back; if you return a *low* card you want the *lower-ranking* suit back. See how it works out, with you sitting in the East seat:

♠ Q J 10   (dummy)
♥ K J 7
♦ K J 10 8 4
♣ 7 4

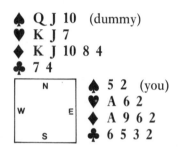

♠ 5 2   (you)
♥ A 6 2
♦ A 9 6 2
♣ 6 5 3 2

This was the bidding:

South	West	North	East
1♠	NB	2♦	NB
3♦	NB	3♠	NB
4♠	NB	NB	NB

Against Four Spades your partner leads ♦ 7. How should you plan the defence? The first thing to strike you is that partner's lead is a singleton and that he will be able to ruff a diamond return after you have taken your Ace. You may wonder how you can be sure that partner has led a singleton rather than a doubleton, but the bidding gives the vital clue. Dummy has five diamonds, you have four, and declarer has *supported his partner's suit*. He must have all three of the cards in the suit that you cannot see, otherwise he would never have raised the diamond bid. Now, you know that your partner is in a position to trump your diamond return, but you have a choice as to which diamond you play back for him to ruff. You must plan ahead. You have a quick re-entry in the Ace of hearts and what you would like partner to do (after ruffing) is to put you in with the heart so that you can give him a second ruff. You can tell him which suit you want back by returning the 9 of diamonds. This will indicate that it is the higher of the other two suits (which are hearts and clubs) that you want back.

If you do not give a suit preference signal, your partner will be faced with a complete guess whether to try a heart or a club. Half the time he will guess wrong and declarer will hasten to draw trumps before your side can score any more ruffs. If you had held the Ace of clubs instead of the Ace of hearts, you would have played back ♦2 at the second trick, directing your partner's attention to the lower-ranking suit, clubs.

THE TRUMP PETER

Normally, as we have seen, a peter in a suit suggests either encouragement or an even number of cards, depending on the circumstances. However, when you are defending against a suit contract a more useful meaning can be attached to a high-low signal in the trump suit itself. It conveys this message: that you had started with exactly three cards in the suit and that *you are interested in trumping something*. It is well worth noting this last point – you do not peter automatically because you have three trumps (sometimes that might be too helpful to declarer!), but only when you have three and *want to ruff*. Often this has the effect of waking partner up – he may not have suspected that you were in a position to score a ruff, but after seeing your signal he will take his time and work out just what it is that you could be interested in trumping.

Suppose that you held this hand:

♠ 8
♥ 10 6 2
♦ J 6 4 3 2
♣ Q 9 7 4

and that you were on lead against a contract of Four Hearts. Sensibly enough you select your singleton spade. Declarer wins this trick and plays the Ace of trumps followed by a low trump to the Queen in dummy which your partner wins with the King. While this has been going on you followed to the Ace with the 6 and to the next heart lead with the 2. Partner then knows that you have a third trump and any doubts he may have had as to whether your spade lead was a singleton or not will have been resolved, for he knows that you are in a position to trump something.

With all these weapons at your disposal, you will find that intelligent defence becomes much easier. One question that is often asked is whether the extensive use of signals can help declarer more than it does the defender's partner. Well, it can happen, but far more often it is the defenders who gain. After all, declarer has a pretty clear picture of his problems and assets from the word go – any additional light that can be shed on the problem will usually benefit the defenders.

CLUES WITHOUT SIGNALS

Before leaving the problems of defence, it is worth thinking about some of the inferences that a defender can draw without the aid of signals from his partner. When explained you may think them over obvious, but it is amazing how even experienced players can fail to add two and two together.

Just suppose that your partner has said No Bid throughout an auction. What inferences can you draw from that? Believe me, this is not a silly question! It could well be that he simply has not got the values for an opening bid, but he might have fair values and have been prevented from bidding:

a. By an opponent's pre-empt.

b. By an opening bid in front of him (he might hold strength in the suit opened, and so have no good call to make).

c. Because the bidding had reached too high a level by the time it was his turn to call.

If, of course, he had the opportunity to open the bidding and yet said No Bid, he is said to have *passed in his own right*, and you know that this is because he simply was not strong enough to open.

Another thought – suppose that you have a particularly weak hand and yet, in spite of silence from your side, the opponents stop short of game and play in a part-score. You can now be sure that partner holds good values but was not able to make a sensible bid.

A final inference that can easily be overlooked is in situations of the following type. Suppose that you have opened the bidding with

One Heart and this has been followed by *two passes*. The opponents end up in Four Spades, you lead the Ace of hearts and these are the cards that you can see in the heart suit:

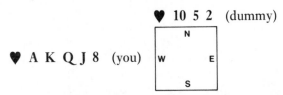

♥ 10 5 2   (dummy)

♥ A K Q J 8   (you)

The Ace of hearts wins the trick and you continue with the King. To your annoyance declarer trumps. It would be very easy to leave it at that, but just stop to think first. Your partner, it appears, held four cards in your suit and yet was unable to raise One Heart to Two Hearts. He must be very weak indeed, certainly less than 6 points, so during the defence you should not rely on him to produce more than a maximum of 5 points in high card strength.

Above all when you are defending, *think* before you play.

17. Counting

Someone once said that the ability to count up to thirteen is all that is needed to play a good game of bridge. Perhaps that is something of an exaggeration, but there is certainly more than a grain of truth in the statement.

Counting at bridge comes under three general headings: counting the missing points, assessing the distribution during the bidding, and assessing the distribution during the play. These ideas can be used by both declarer and the defenders, as the following examples will show.

First, take a very simple situation – so simple that it hardly seems worth including, but one which nevertheless illustrates an important line of thinking that is easy to overlook. Suppose that an opponent has opened the bidding with 1NT but that, in spite of the adverse opening, you and your partner end in a game. Dummy comes down and as declarer you find that you have 27 honour points in the combined hands. That you have got plenty for game will be your first thought, but don't stop there! You should also realise that every single one of the outstanding 13 points are with the opponent who opened 1NT, and you will undoubtedly be able to take advantage of your knowledge during the play. With a suit like this:

K 10 3

A J 2

if it was *East* who had bid 1NT, you would tackle the play by leading low from the North hand and finessing the Jack. However, if it was West who had bid 1NT, you would lead the 2 from the South hand with a view to finessing North's 10. This would be a two-way finesse from which every element of guess-work had been removed.

Even if, after the same opening of 1NT, your side had ended in a part score with only 23 points between the two hands, it would still be long odds in favour of finding the missing Queen with the opening bidder. A player who is *known* to hold 13 or 14 points is far more likely to hold a particular high card than his partner who is known to hold 3 or 4 points.

ASSESSING DISTRIBUTION FROM OPPONENTS' BIDDING

The opponents' bidding can also be extremely helpful to you in forming a picture of their hands. Say that they have bid as follows:

West	*East*
1♦	1♠
2♥	2NT
3♥	4♥

What impression have you formed of West's hand after this sequence of bidding? That he has a lot of red cards in his hand? Good, but you can be more precise than that. Firstly, West has got *more* diamonds than hearts for he has reversed. Secondly, he has at least five hearts as he has rebid the suit. So you know that he has at least six diamonds and five hearts. That accounts for eleven of his thirteen cards and he cannot possibly have more than two cards in spades and clubs. So far, you have no idea whether he has started with a singleton in both black suits or a doubleton in one and a void in the other, but if the early play reveals that he holds two spades, it will not be too difficult to place him with a void in clubs.

I cannot resist including at this stage a hand that I myself played in a Gold Cup match – it illustrates the above ideas well.

These were the North–South cards:

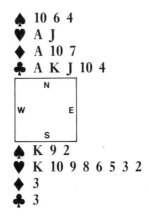

♠ 10 6 4
♥ A J
♦ A 10 7
♣ A K J 10 4

♠ K 9 2
♥ K 10 9 8 6 5 3 2
♦ 3
♣ 3

North dealt, with East-West vulnerable and opened One Club. East over-called with One Diamond and as South I made a pre-emptive bid of Four Hearts. West and North passed but East fought on with Four Spades. I passed, West passed, and North, with the feeling that he had been a bit too cautious on the last round of bidding, jumped to Six Hearts which became the final contract.

Against Six Hearts West led ♠8. East won with the Ace and returned ♠Q to my King, West following suit. At this point I needed all the remaining tricks. There were three trumps missing: the Queen, the 7 and the 4. One would usually play small to the Ace and hope that they were divided 2-1, but here the bidding had been very informative. East, who was vulnerable, had first bid diamonds and then spades at the Four level. He could hardly join in at that level with only a four card suit, so he was marked with five spades. But he had bid diamonds first, so presumably his diamonds were longer than his spades. So that marked him with eleven cards in spades and diamonds and left room for only two cards in the other suits. Rather than commit myself to an immediate guess in trumps, I led a club to the Ace at trick 3. When East followed suit, I played another top club and again East followed.

East's missing two cards had been accounted for and it was like playing with all four hands exposed on the table. I trumped a club in hand, then led a low heart and finessed dummy's Jack. As expected East showed out and I had the remaining tricks.

ASSESSING DISTRIBUTION DURING THE PLAY

Sometimes you will be given no help at all by the opponent's bidding – they will remain silent throughout the auction, and you will have to rely on inferences from the play to place missing cards. With a sight of all four hands this is easy, but remember that when declarer plays the hand below he can see only his own hand and dummy. And yet, as the play progresses, he can make his contract a certainty.

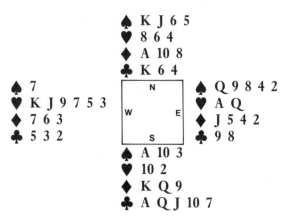

```
                    ♠ K J 6 5
                    ♥ 8 6 4
                    ♦ A 10 8
                    ♣ K 6 4
  ♠ 7                              ♠ Q 9 8 4 2
  ♥ K J 9 7 5 3     N              ♥ A Q
  ♦ 7 6 3        W     E           ♦ J 5 4 2
  ♣ 5 3 2           S              ♣ 9 8
                    ♠ A 10 3
                    ♥ 10 2
                    ♦ K Q 9
                    ♣ A Q J 10 7
```

With silent opponents, North–South reached a contract of Five Clubs and West led ♥7. As usual, declarer counted his top winners: there were five clubs, three diamonds and two spades, giving ten tricks. However, the defenders were in a position to take only two immediate tricks, both in hearts. The fate of the contract depended on whether declarer could locate the missing Queen of spades. The spade suit offered a two-way finesse and, at first glance, a successful guess would provide an eleventh trick while a poor guess would give the defenders their third trick to defeat the Five Clubs contract. One thing was certain; there was no hurry to finesse in spades and declarer set out to see what information he could gain about the opponents' hands. East won the opening lead with ♥A and returned ♥Q. As he knew that his partner held no more hearts, West overtook the Queen with his King and continued with a third round of hearts, ruffed by declarer, while East discarded a low spade. So at this point South knew that West had started with six hearts and East with only two. South next drew all of the opposing trumps in three rounds and elicited the information that West had started with three cards in the suit. There was still no hurry to commit himself in spades so declarer continued by cashing the three top diamonds, *to all of which West followed suit*. So now twelve of West's thirteen cards were known to declarer – he had started with six hearts, three clubs and three diamonds and could have at most one spade. All guesswork related to the spade situation had disappeared; South led the 3 of spades to dummy's King and, when West followed suit with a low spade, was able to finesse ♠ 10 on the next round with total confidence. By careful counting South had been able to improve a 50% guess to a 100% certainty.

DEFENSIVE COUNTING

The principles of counting that have been discussed above can also be applied by a defender. Imagine yourself in the West seat on the deal below, defending against 3NT by South:

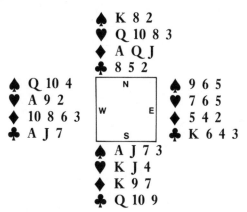

This was the bidding:

South	West	North	East
1NT	NB	2♣ *a*	NB
2♠ *b*	NB	2NT *c*	NB
3NT *d*	NB	NB	NB

a. Stayman, asking for four card major suits.
b. Admitting to four spades, but denying a four-card heart suit.

c. With no interest in spades, but quite happy to play in 2NT even if partner has minimum for his 1NT bid.

d. With a full 14 points, South is happy to go on to game.

What conclusions can you, as West, draw from the bidding? You can infer that North has twelve points (he was interested in game, but not sufficiently sure to bid it himself) and that South, who accepted the invitation to go on, must have 14 points. You also know that South's hand includes four spades, but not four hearts and that North (who used Stayman) presumably has got four hearts. For the moment, however, there is nothing clever to be done and you lead the fourth highest of your longest suit – the 3 of diamonds. Declarer plays the Jack from the table and this wins – your partner discouraging firmly by playing the 2, thus marking South with the King. At trick 2 declarer leads ♥3 from dummy and plays the King from his own hand. Sensibly enough, you hold up for the time being – it is possible that by waiting you may get some clues as to where the five tricks that you need to defeat 3NT are coming from. South continues with ♥J and a third heart which you are forced to win. It is still not clear what you should do for the best – the lead of either a club or a spade *could* be just what declarer wants to give him his ninth trick, so for the time being it is probably safest to play another diamond – it is just possible that you will eventually establish the thirteenth card in the suit as a trick. Declarer wins on the table, plays off ♠K which wins the trick, and continues with a finesse of ♠J. You win with the Queen and now is the moment of decision. It is true that you can indeed establish a trick in diamonds, but have you got time for it?

What picture have you formed of declarer's hand so far? It appears that he started with four spades (he bid the suit in reply to Stayman) headed by the Ace and Jack (your partner cannot hold the Ace or he would have taken dummy's King), three hearts headed by the King and Jack, and you know he has the King of diamonds. So if you quietly play another diamond, South will make three diamonds, three hearts and three spades (for you know the suit is breaking 3–3 for declarer), and that will give him nine tricks and his contract. You must ask yourself whether there is room in your partner's hand for the King of clubs. Count South's points. He has shown up with 5 in spades, 4 in hearts and 3 in diamonds –

that makes 12 points! The Queen of clubs must be in his hand to make up the 14 points you know he started with, but he cannot have ♣K, for then he would have been too strong (with 15 points) to have opened 1NT.

So far the defence has taken two tricks – to defeat the contract it is necessary to take three more. It will do no good to lead ♣A and follow with a club to partner's King, for in that case declarer will make a trick with his Queen of clubs. The only way to do it is to lead a *low* club to partner's marked King, then on the club return you will have the Ace–Jack tenace sitting over the Queen in South's hand – a guarantee of two more tricks. At the point when you found the killing switch to a low club you had a complete picture of declarer's hand – not all the low cards of course, but everything that mattered.

ONE LAST CHANCE

Finally, although the hand has not really got anything to do with the ideas of counting that we have been discussing, the following deal might give you just a hint of the sort of possibilities that lie ahead of you in this game.

Try your luck on this hand. Imagine that you are playing in Six Hearts against the opening lead of the Queen of spades.

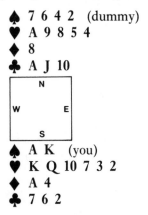

♠ 7 6 4 2 (dummy)
♥ A 9 8 5 4
♦ 8
♣ A J 10

♠ A K (you)
♥ K Q 10 7 3 2
♦ A 4
♣ 7 6 2

With no losers in spades, hearts or diamonds it looks as though the success of your contract will depend entirely on avoiding two losers in clubs. At first sight there is no better play than to take a double finesse in clubs – a play that will fail, albeit unluckily, if East has started with both the King and Queen of clubs. However, there is a way in which you, as South, can make 100% certain of your contract. It is with what is called an *elimination play*. The idea is that before you take any finesses in clubs you will have eliminated all the side suit cards from both your hand and dummy. The play should go like this: after winning the lead with ♠A, play off ♥K and ♥Q, drawing all of the outstanding trumps. Then follow with ♠K, the Ace of diamonds, and a diamond ruff in dummy. Next comes a spade ruff in hand, then you cross to dummy with ♥A and ruff the last spade. Now, with the elimination complete, you take a club finesse. If it loses to East, this is your position:

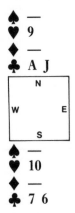

Now, East is on lead. What can he do to you? A club return is right into the **A J** in dummy and gives you the remaining tricks. And it will do him no good to play a spade or a diamond if he has one left, for all you need do is throw your losing club from hand and ruff on the table. He will have been forced to concede a ruff and discard, making a play that gives you a trick, however the cards lie.

One of the reasons why bridge is such a fascinating game is that no two hands are ever exactly alike. Furthermore, no matter how bad your hand, you still have an active interest in the play. Even if your opponents bid confidently to a small slam, a target of twelve tricks, your aim in life, with your partner's co-operation, is to come to two tricks and so defeat their slam. The only time that you can really relax is when you are dummy! And even then, you will want to keep an eye open on partner's activities in case he shows signs of revoking or leading from the wrong hand and you have a chance to draw his attention to the matter.

I hope that you have not got the idea that now you have reached the last chapter you have mastered everything that there is to be mastered in the game! Far from it; but at least you have a sensible grounding. Anything that you can do involving bridge is good for your game, whether it is playing, watching, reading books, reading newspaper articles or (not least!) watching television programmes on the game.